LEADING

A leader's guide to mental health conversations at work

WELLBEING

Fleur Heazlewood

MAJOR STREET

First published in 2023 by Major Street Publishing Pty Ltd
E: info@majorstreet.com.au W: majorstreet.com.au M: +61 421 707 983

© Fleur Heazlewood 2023
The moral rights of the author have been asserted.

A catalogue record for this book is available from
the National Library of Australia

Printed book ISBN: 978-1-922611-77-2
Ebook ISBN: 978-1-922611-78-9

Cover design by Tess McCabe
Internal design by Production Works
Printed in Australia by Griffin Press

10 9 8 7 6 5 4 3 2 1

PRAISE FOR *LEADING WELLBEING*

'Every leader should have this book in their toolkit. If you manage people and find the topic of mental health overwhelming but increasingly important, then this book is full of sound advice, relatable stories and easy-to-digest, practical ways to help you and your team feel supported as you navigate these conversations. Fleur's solid leadership background and lived experience of managing the mental wellbeing of herself and her teams, combined with her award-winning writing, means this is a book I will certainly turn to again and again.'
Sonja Furniss, Senior People Program Manager

'*Leading Wellbeing* really speaks to me. Fleur is so honest and real in sharing her journey and exploring how to manage those difficult mental health conversations while having strategies in place to protect your own wellbeing. Her approach to leading and promoting wellbeing is inspiring. This is a great book that really made me stop and think about how to manage my own wellbeing while supporting others.'
Narelle Wallace, Director, Australian Public Service

'All people leaders need to be competent engaging their people in mental health conversations. Mental health conversations are peppered with many imagined and real pitfalls, and without a map to navigate those pitfalls it's easier to avoid the conversations that need to be had. *Leading Wellbeing* is the map; so, thanks to Fleur, every worker can engage in authentic mental health conversations to help boost wellbeing and productivity at work.'
Eugene McGarrell, Health Executive (Mental Health Service Development and Performance) and Board Director.

'*Leading Wellbeing* contains a wealth of practical guidance for supporting the mental health of individuals and teams in a post-pandemic world. Whether you are leading a team of high-flying lawyers or a kids' sport team, the framework and guidance of Leading Wellbeing will make you more effective by improving your capacity to support and nurture others.'
Barry Hemsley, Assistant Director, Australian Public Service

'This book is an amazing resource for those in need of a practical and actionable guide to identifying and supporting those they lead who may be struggling with mental health.'
Colleen O'Connor, Head of HR

CONTENTS

About the author   vii

Acknowledgements   ix

Introduction   1

How to use this book   5

PART I: THE STATE OF PLAY   9

Chapter 1: People are not okay   13

Chapter 2: Our role   33

Chapter 3: See the signs   51

Chapter 4: Self-assessment   63

PART II: THE MENTAL HEALTH MASTERY
FRAMEWORK   81

Chapter 5: Prepare   85

Chapter 6: Ask   99

Chapter 7: Listen   111

Chapter 8: Empower   121

Chapter 9: Performance   131

Bringing it all together: Mental Health Mastery   143

Connect with me   153

References   157

Resources   161

ABOUT THE AUTHOR

Fleur Heazlewood is a leadership expert, keynote speaker and founder of the Blueberry Institute.

Fleur partners with leaders to create healthy, high-performing teams and organisations. She is known for building positive performance cultures that deliver both employee wellbeing and commercial results. She has trained and mentored over 3000 people in positive leadership, future-fit resilience and mental health mastery.

With over 20 years' corporate leadership experience, she has led many successful organisational turnarounds and culture transformations. Fleur understands first-hand the challenges of change, uncertainty, staff stress and top talent burnout. Her clients value her accessibility, practicality and skilled use of lessons that work in real life.

Fleur works with many high-profile organisations, including the Australian Government Department of Veterans' Affairs, Woolworths, GenesisCare, ITW Construction, Axicom, Goodman Fielder, Indara, Mental Health Commission of New South Wales, the Australian Government Department of Finance and the Country Fire Authority.

Fleur's experience is backed by extensive qualifications, which include a Masters of Coaching Psychology, Bachelor of

Commerce and Company Directors Certificate. She is a qualified yoga therapy and mindfulness teacher and incorporates this in her personal wellbeing and healing practices.

Her debut book *Resilience Recipes* won best Health and Wellbeing Book of 2022 at the Australian Business Book Awards and was a runner up for Business Book of the Year.

ACKNOWLEDGEMENTS

Leadership is a constant balancing act, and it's natural to feel pulled in different directions. As leaders, it is important to remember that you are human, too, and to know it is okay to ask for help and take time for self-care.

Much gratitude to my team, who are also my friends and cheer squad. They support and celebrate me and each other through the good, wobbly, great and awful ups and downs in life. Chloe, Jodie, Stephen, Meaveen and Nick bring a richness of unique gifts, perspectives, strengths and vulnerabilities that makes our work and our team wonderful to be a part of. Thank you also to Yarden, who chose to intern with us as part of her studies and painstakingly researched and checked the facts, stats and international content for mental health.

True growth and reaching our full potential as leaders occurs when we take personal risks, share our vulnerabilities, admit when we don't have the answers and ask for help.

This book wouldn't have been possible without the hundreds of leaders who have been willing to ask the scary, uncertain, silly and ultimately brave questions in my mental health, resilience and wellbeing workshops in order to better support their people.

Special thanks to Sonja, Barry, Tammy, Narelle, Barsha, Mike, Jane, Colleen and Victoria for your belief, feedback and ongoing support.

Leading with psychological safety is also about having the courage to advocate for what you believe is right, be open to a range of ideas and perspectives, and support people's voices to be heard.

Much gratitude to Eugene McGarrell and Lou Bentley for your friendship, belief and backing. Eugene has been an important part of my ten-plus-year journey in bringing mental health and wellbeing literacy to the world of work. Big thanks for the mental health expertise feedback provided during the development of *Leading Wellbeing*. Lou has a big heart, enormous 'energi' and a great talent for message and marketing. Thank you for your generous support in sharing the message of better wellbeing for work and amplifying my leadership voice.

Positive leadership that leads to sustainable performance is possible for any team when we start supporting wellbeing and building resilience as a capability and enabler of performance, rather than as a reward for results.

I acknowledge the leaders who, during the formative part of my career, demonstrated care for me as a person as well as appreciation for the results I delivered: Mark Bilton, Kim Gosper and Brian Jewell. I also acknowledge the leaders I have had the privilege of working with who have both the vision and commitment to build wellbeing as a foundation of a healthy, high-performing culture: Gavan McKenna and Mike Riches.

And finally, a big thank you to my winning book team, who have chosen to work with me a second time. They were invaluable in helping me write my debut book *Resilience Recipes*.

Thank you to Kelly, for challenging me to do better and pressure-testing the book idea and structure; to Lesley, Will and Eleanor at Major Street Publishing for helping bring the book to life; and Tess McCabe for another gorgeous cover design.

INTRODUCTION

You are exhausted from the continuous juggle of day-to-day business priorities, delivering on urgent work deadlines and supporting an under-resourced team that is cracking under the unrelenting pressure.

You take on more of the team's workload in an attempt to shield your people from some of the more unrealistic work demands and relieve some of their stress burden. But no matter how hard you work at it, you don't feel as though you ever get on top of things. You feel caught in a no-win downward spiral that you don't know how to break.

This book is for leaders who want to do their best but worry about how to better manage the demands of the business with the health and wellbeing of their team. You are not alone – and this book is here to help.

This book is for leaders who are willing to be courageous and embrace the conversational skills needed to better support the mental health and wellbeing of their people at work.

LEADERSHIP MATTERS

As leaders, healthy change starts with us. And it is not just what we say but also what we do that matters.

In the healthy leadership programs I run, I have learned that leading with courage, with vulnerable personal sharing, creates the psychological safety and trust necessary to have the caring conversations that count. When I lead workshops with my lived experience, there is greater openness within the group – the burning questions are asked, the quality of the conversation deepens, and people listen with curiosity and respond to each other with compassion.

So, to encourage you to lead with courage and model vulnerability, I will share some of my personal, raw stories and why I care so deeply about leaders developing mental health mastery for work.

I started my career as a bright, ambitious young woman during a time when equal opportunity, flexibility, fair work and discrimination laws, policies and protections didn't really exist. During my first year of work I was bullied, harassed, ridiculed, threatened, sexually assaulted and ostracised for being young, female, qualified, competent and different. I started my working career in a tough employment market, and if I could have found a job anywhere else, I would have taken it.

The leaders who I turned to for help with this psychological harm pleaded helplessness and then, behind my back, contributed to the rumour mill that I was trouble. My manager distanced themself from me because they saw me as a threat to their career progression. I was ostracised by my team and left to figure out how to be safe on my own.

I shut down and focused on survival. I worked twice as hard as everyone else to continuously justify my existence.

My days were spent living in my stress response and on adrenaline, and dreading Mondays. Weekends were spent in a state of mental exhaustion, and expensive health-retreat holidays were dedicated to finding new and faster ways to recover and manage burnout.

When I eventually resigned, it was as one of the company's top performers. The leaders scrambled to create incentives for me to stay. I didn't.

Ill health is not an acceptable price for business success.

MENTAL HEALTH MASTERY IS AN ESSENTIAL PART OF YOUR LEADERSHIP TOOLKIT

Most of us move into leadership and management roles with clarity around the tasks, projects, targets and results we are expected to deliver. There is an investment in training and time dedicated to work-in-progress meetings, either one-on-one or in teams, and performance expectations come with a range of measures for assessing our levels of performance and success.

Less explicit and often more informal, unwritten and unmeasured is an assumption that we will also manage the wellbeing of our team within the cracks of our leftover time. But when we don't manage the interpersonal dynamics well, leave those who are unwell to struggle, allow interpersonal conflict to fester or accept poor performance, we undermine both our own health and performance and that of our overall team.

High performance is not sustainable unless it is *healthy* high performance.

The leadership wisdom in this book comes from my lived experience struggling with burnout, fluctuating mental health and a relentless drive for high performance. I worked extremely hard and fast-tracked a successful corporate career that took me from graduate trainee in a blue-chip global company to CEO of a multi-million-dollar business in just 15 years.

I overachieved on every commercial performance measure given to me, but I existed in a perpetual state of burnout – and ended up damaging both my mental health and physical health along the way.

There is a better way, and this book will help you find it.

MENTAL HEALTH IS EVERYONE'S BUSINESS

Mental health is something that we all experience, but when we notice someone struggling at work, we hope that Human Resources (HR) or someone else will deal with it. But with one in five of us experiencing mental illness at work each year, we all have a role to play in supporting our colleagues. With work being where we spend so many of our waking hours, the relationships with our direct managers and team members are some of the most significant influences on our mental health and wellbeing.

We don't have to be experts in mental health to have a caring conversation that connects someone who needs help to support. While this book has 'mental health' in the subtitle, the heart of it is about helping you to have better conversations at work – conversations that connect rather than disconnect, and that enable you to feel more confident offering timely and appropriate support to team members who may be struggling. It is as simple as starting one small conversation at a time.

Applying the Mental Health Mastery Framework to improve the conversations you are already having will alleviate worry and stress without adding to your workload. And research shows that people who feel valued and supported at work perform better, are more engaged and stay longer.

People who are well do well.

HOW TO USE THIS BOOK

This book provides you with a conversation framework to help you more confidently and capably have better mental health and wellbeing conversations at work as a leader. With just a little bit of preparation, and utilising your existing meeting calendar, you can make a positive difference to people's mental health and performance without adding much to your workload.

This book should feel a lot like common sense – because it is. It is simple and deliberately curated to minimise your mental load and help you make small positive changes to your conversations at work. This is a practical book with examples, scripts and checklists to help you prepare for conversations that better connect and support.

Take this book at your own pace. Each chapter is designed to build on the last, but this book doesn't have to be worked through sequentially. If one area resonates with you more, go there, read it and commit to an action.

This book will help you to recognise when someone may be experiencing mental health challenges and could benefit from support. It provides ideas, strategies and tips for how you can have better and more supportive wellbeing conversations with people you are concerned about at work. It is designed to improve the mental health literacy of leaders and teams in the workplace, to reduce stigma and to increase help-seeking for those who are unwell.

What I am sharing with you comes from my lived experience with mental illness, personal burnout, healing journey, years of study and leadership experience. It also comes from the conversations I have had in training over 3000 leaders across a range of industries, states and countries in my programs on mental health mastery, future-fit resilience skills and positive leadership.

WHAT THIS BOOK COVERS

Part I of this book provides your leadership context and the opportunity for you to create a personal development plan based on a short self-assessment.

In chapters one to three, I define the key terms you need to know, cover your leadership responsibilities for psychological safety and provide warning signs of burnout and potential mental health problems. Chapter four provides a self-assessment for you to determine your personal development plan starting point when it comes to your confidence and competence in supporting the mental health of your team at work.

Part II of this book covers the practical strategies and steps that address the most common challenges leaders face when having a mental health conversation at work. It addresses how to approach someone you are concerned about at work, how to start a mental health conversation, what to say in response to personal disclosure and how to help.

In chapters five to nine, we work through the five steps of the Mental Health Mastery Framework – Prepare, Ask, Listen, Empower and Performance – to build your conversation competence and confidence.

Supporting your people to be well will also help them to do well and ultimately achieve both healthy and high performance.

WHAT THIS BOOK IS NOT

I am not a psychologist, therapist or counsellor. I am not an expert in workplace HR and safety policy, processes and regulations. This book does not teach, constitute advice or qualify you to diagnose, prescribe, recommend treatment or take specific courses of action. That is the clear role of mental health and medical professionals. Nor does this book replace the valuable guidance that your HR, wellbeing and safety teams, professional helplines and employee assistance programs (EAPs) that are relevant to your organisation provide.

Different states, territories, cultures and countries have different guidelines, policies and regulations when it comes to psychological safety and mental health at work. It is important that you familiarise yourself with the policies applicable to your organisation, the relevant protocols for your culture and regulations that govern your geographical location.

PART I

THE STATE
OF PLAY

MENTAL ILL HEALTH is largely undetectable. It is not easy to see, and yet it is more common than many of us realise.

When you look at the line-up of people at work in Figure 1, can you pick which two currently have a diagnosable mental illness? One is experiencing mood swings with anxiety, and sometimes has frightening panic attacks. Another struggling with depression finds it so difficult to get out of bed in the morning that they are often late to work or miss work altogether some days.

Figure 1: Who is suffering from mental ill health?

Can you see the two people experiencing mental health pressure? Which person is exhausted and not sleeping due to disruptive caring responsibilities for an active toddler and a parent with dementia? Which person has a family history of substance addiction and is worried about a sibling's overuse of alcohol?

Can you identify the two stressed leaders? There is a supervisor who is concerned about two of their people and shouldering extra workload to take pressure off them, pushing themselves towards burnout in the process. There is also a team leader trying to work out a return-to-work plan for a staff member who has lost confidence after six months' leave managing a mental health condition.

Our overarching responsibility as leaders is to promote psychological safety, provide a healthy working environment and provide support for people with mental health challenges.

Mental health mastery is no longer a nice-to-have; it is a necessary part of your leadership toolkit.

In Part I of this book, we define what mental health is, cover what your responsibilities are for providing a psychologically safe working environment and identify the warning signs for burnout and potential mental health problems.

You will have the opportunity to do a self-assessment of your starting point when it comes to your confidence and competence in supporting mental health at work. This will help you choose your focus for development with the Mental Health Mastery Framework in Part II.

Mental health conversation competence helps leaders strengthen their relationships with their teams, leading to improved communication, collaboration and overall performance.

CHAPTER 1

PEOPLE ARE NOT OKAY

People are under pressure. Pressure from external events such as the pandemic, country conflicts, natural disasters such as flooding and bushfires, and economic uncertainty are exacerbating mental health issues around the globe.

In my discussions with leaders, the best way I have found to bring mental health issues to life is by defining the context with definitions, facts and stories of lived experience.

There was a small team of ten people that worked together in a local office supporting a range of departments across their organisation. They were capable and experienced in their separate fields, but some of them were struggling with mental health issues.

One member of the team, Ella, had been diagnosed with depression a few months ago. She was finding it difficult to concentrate and complete her work on time. Ella was exhausting herself with constant worry about her future and job security.

Another team member, Tom, had been dealing with anxiety for several years. He found it hard to communicate with his colleagues and often avoided social events. His anxiety also made him doubt his abilities and be reluctant to take on new responsibilities.

Meanwhile, Ollie was going through a difficult divorce. Ollie's personal life was impacting his work, and he was finding it challenging to stay focused.

The rest of the team was not aware of the struggles that Ella, Tom and Ollie were living. They knew their colleagues were not performing as well as they used to but attributed it to laziness and lack of motivation.

Mental health challenges are natural and common, not niche. In any 12-month period, 20% of adults experience a diagnosable mental illness. That amounts to one in five people in our teams at work each year who are not okay.

Mental health risk at work is real. Mental health is a growing safety risk in the workplace, with the workplace being cited as a primary source of stress, and more than 90% of Australia's mental health compensation claims are linked to work-related stress or mental stress. The three most common causes of mental stress are preventable and relate to a lack of psychological safety at work. They are:

1. work pressure (31%)
2. work-related harassment and/or bullying (27%)
3. exposure to workplace or occupational violence (14%).

Ignorance is no longer an excuse. Federal legislation in Australia mandates that employers manage psychosocial hazards under the Work Health and Safety Act. Other countries are reviewing and updating their legislation.

Organisations are now expected to create mentally healthy workplaces and protect the mental health of their employees. As leaders, that translates to a legal responsibility to ensure that we are providing people with a working environment that is not just physically safe but also psychologically safe.

Whitney worked as a project manager for a large organisation. She loved her job and enjoyed working with her colleagues. However, one of her project team colleagues, Noah, had been bullying her for several months. He would make derogatory comments about Whitney's work and appearance and would exclude her from important meetings. Whitney tried to ignore Noah's behaviour, but it was becoming increasingly difficult. She spoke to her manager about her challenges with Noah, and her manager suggested that she needed to learn to be more assertive.

With the project delivery deadline fast approaching, the stress of the situation was taking a toll on Whitney's mental health. She was having trouble sleeping and continually felt anxious. Whitney found it difficult to concentrate at work and was losing confidence from being cut out of meetings and making mistakes on her projects. Whitney felt isolated and alone and didn't know where to turn for help.

As leaders, what we say and do – or don't say and don't do – makes a key contribution to the mental health and psychological safety of our team members.

STIGMA AND STRUGGLING

The biggest barrier people with mental health problems face at work is stigma.

Stigma is defined as a deeply discrediting attitude that reduces individuals 'from a whole and usual person to a tainted, discounted one'. Research shows that either stigma or the fear of stigma can cause people experiencing mental health difficulties to avoid seeking or receiving treatment. Unfortunately, negative attitudes and beliefs towards people who have a mental health condition are common.

More than 50% of people with a common, diagnosable mental illness do not receive professional help. So, people are struggling on their own who don't need to be. And research shows that the earlier someone connects with help, the easier and shorter their healing journey is likely to be.

Ethan had been in his role for five years. He was a diligent employee, always putting in long hours and going above and beyond for his clients. Behind the diligence, Ethan was hiding his struggle with depression. Over time Ethan's mental health deteriorated, exacerbated by the effort it took to pretend to be healthy for his colleagues and work the extra hours to prove his worth.

Ethan was worried that if he revealed his mental illness, his supervisor, colleagues and superiors would think less of him and his career prospects would be negatively impacted.

Ethan was struggling to concentrate at work and found it increasingly hard to get out of bed in the morning.

He knew he needed help but didn't know what to do, and he was worried that taking sick leave would invite unwanted questions.

There is a vast range of reasons why people may not feel comfortable or safe accepting professional help, or worthy of it. There are also cultural considerations, which are diverse and too nuanced to do justice to here and so are not covered in this book, but there are some great community resources available.

Particularly when we talk about mental health at work, we can group the barriers that people face in reaching out for help into two broad categories:

1. personal reasons
2. workplace reasons.

Personal reasons can be wide-ranging. Examples include:

- fear of stigma and rejection by friends, family or their community
- shame or embarrassment – thinking that they should be able to cope because everyone else seems to be fine
- the fact that mental health problems often build over time, and so someone may not recognise they need help
- lack of education in understanding the signs, options for help and professional supports available
- lack of accessible and confidential professional help options, particularly in regional or remote areas
- the cost of professional help
- poor treatment or experience in the past, either personally or of someone they know.

There are also specific work-related barriers. Examples include:

- fear of stigma and rejection by colleagues, peers, direct reports and managers
- cultural norms and expectations, such as an expectation to adopt a 'stiff upper lip' and 'put your game face on' or 'suck it up, buttercup'
- performance management concerns – worry about job security and negative performance ratings
- fear of discrimination – worry about their job being downgraded or being passed over for a promotion they would otherwise be considered for
- feeling isolated
- worrying about being ostracised by their colleagues
- lack of supporting policies and procedures for flexibility, reasonable adjustments and support
- poor workplace treatment in the past, either in a previous workplace or in the current workplace
- financial concerns, such as not enough sick leave or annual leave to take time off without causing financial stress.

As leaders, we can reduce the influence of stigma by recognising that it is natural for people to experience mental health ups and downs – to make it okay for people in our teams to share when they are not okay, and to show empathy, respect and support for people who are struggling.

DEFINITIONS MATTER

We fear what we don't know, and by drawing a map of the terrain and providing shape and context we can take away some of the uncertainty that comes with difficult conversations.

So, before we discuss how to better support people experiencing mental health challenges at work, it is important to improve our understanding of the key terms most often used. Terms such as 'mental health', 'mental illness', 'stress' and 'burnout' mean different things to different people. Each of these mental health challenges is also experienced uniquely depending on our individual mix of factors, such as life experiences, biology, coping strategies, support networks, education and access to services.

Before we can provide better health and wellbeing support, we need to appreciate what contributes to good mental wellbeing.

What is mental health?

Many people associate the term 'mental health' with poor mental health or mental illness. But mental health actually refers to a positive state. Mental health is defined by the World Health Organization as 'a state of well-being in which the individual realizes his or her own abilities, can cope with the normal stresses of life, can work productively and fruitfully, and is able to make a contribution to his or her community'.

Good mental health or mental wellbeing is characterised by:

- feeling relatively confident in yourself with positive self-esteem
- feeling and expressing a range of emotions
- building and maintaining good relationships with others
- feeling engaged with the world in general
- living and working productively
- coping with the stresses of daily life, including work-related stress
- adapting and managing in times of change and uncertainty.

Mental health is experienced on a continuum

An individual's mental health can be considered to sit somewhere along a continuum, with good mental health at one end and poor mental health at the other (see Figure 2).

Mental health is not static. An individual's position will shift throughout their life (or even a single day) depending on the situations they face and the range of socioeconomic, biological and environmental factors they experience.

Figure 2: The mental health continuum

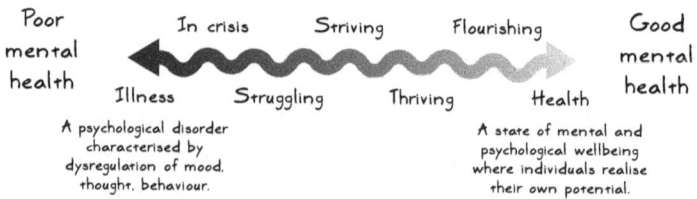

Poor mental health

In crisis   Striving   Flourishing

Illness   Struggling   Thriving   Health

Good mental health

A psychological disorder characterised by dysregulation of mood, thought, behaviour.

A state of mental and psychological wellbeing where individuals realise their own potential.

It is both natural and normal to have ups and downs and to shift along the continuum from time to time. For example, someone might feel really stressed out when moving house or starting a new job. This is not a sign of clinical anxiety but a one-off, reasonable reaction to the situation they are facing. The stress resolves when the situation resolves.

Poor mental health can be considered a state in which thinking, feeling or reacting becomes difficult or even impossible to cope with. Mental illness refers to a psychological disorder diagnosed by professionals and characterised by dysregulation of mood, thought and/or behaviour.

> As leaders, it is important for us to understand that someone experiencing mental illness will, most of the time, function well at work with support and professional help.

Stress is a natural part of life

Stress has the potential to negatively affect our mental health if not managed well.

Stress is how you react when you feel under pressure or threatened. When you are stressed, your body releases stress hormones such as adrenaline. This brings on physical changes in your body that help you respond to the stressful situation.

The body's stress response may also be called the 'fight, flight or freeze' response and is a helpful way your body has adapted to respond to danger. When you experience episodes of stress, the stress hormones your body releases keep you alert and able to face challenges.

Andy was an engineer working on a high-pressure project with a tight deadline. Andy was a hardworking, dedicated employee, but the pressure and stress of the project was starting to take a toll on their mental and physical health. They began experiencing symptoms of stress, such as difficulty sleeping, loss of appetite and irritability.

Andy found it increasingly hard to concentrate and cover the numerous tasks that were becoming urgent. Andy's stress levels were also causing physical symptoms, such as headaches and muscle tension, which made it difficult to think and function well.

The project was completed and successfully delivered to the client on time. Andy felt a tremendous sense of relief and accomplishment, and their stress levels dropped significantly. Andy was able to sleep better, eat normally and feel more relaxed and at ease.

Stress is a normal reaction to everyday pressures but can become unhealthy when it disrupts your day-to-day functioning. While everyone will feel stress at times, each person's experience is different. Knowing what your stress triggers are and how you respond to different challenges in life will help you manage stressful periods.

WORK AND STRESS

Work-related stress has been specifically defined by the World Health Organization as the 'response people may have when presented with demands and pressures that are not matched to their abilities, leading to an inability to cope, especially when they feel they have little support from supervisors and little control over work processes'.

As leaders, we are responsible for ensuring that our people have the clarity, training, support, resources, knowledge, feedback and supervision they require to perform their jobs healthily and well.

A mentally healthy environment is one in which leaders protect, respond to and promote mental health for their people.

Gemma, Andy's manager, recognised the elevated levels of stress in the team and took steps to better balance the workload and provide additional support where needed. Gemma arranged for team members to work in pairs, scheduled regular breaks and supported them to prioritise self-care.

Stress becomes a mental health problem when it lasts a long time, or if you feel overwhelmed and unable to cope with your situation. While stress is not a mental illness in and of itself, prolonged stress may lead to mental health issues or burnout. It is important that you prioritise your self-care and health.

LET'S TALK ABOUT BURNOUT

I was the head of a homewares business and oversaw design, overseas procurement, local manufacturing and distribution across all of Australia's major retailers. I reported to the Group Managing Director and the Board of the parent company, which included my predecessor.

My predecessor was paid a handsome fee to manage the business transition of leadership. He made it clear that he saw this retainer as a core part of his retirement income, so it was in his best interests to publicly undermine my competence with my company and the Board so he would still be needed. This included secret meetings with my Finance Manager, who was resentful that she wasn't CEO. She refused to give me current financials and would only provide accurate financial reports to the Board at our monthly Board Meetings, where my predecessor would routinely humiliate me.

At the end of every working day, I stayed back to work on my own spreadsheets and models, and double-check purchase orders and factory instructions. Weeks turned into months, and I didn't notice when 70-hour working weeks became my new norm.

When the global financial crisis hit, our product orders were cancelled by the major department stores and our sales dried up literally overnight. I didn't have anyone at work who I could trust to talk things through with, and I knew that I would have to figure out how to navigate this on my own.

Every day for 18 months, I absorbed the stress and questions of 100 good people worried about the lack of work and their job security. Every decision I made became the difference between someone having enough work or losing their job. I took on my people's stress as my own.

I wasn't sleeping, with my overactive mind stuck in a 24/7 problem-solving cycle. Living with exhaustion, getting out of bed each morning was a battle. Existing on cortisol and adrenaline, I made it through each day with litres of caffeine and sugar.

I was easily irritated, quick to tear up over silly things and struggling to manage intense mood swings. Most weeks I was at the doctor with colds, stomach pains, skin inflammations and unrelenting headaches. I spent a small fortune on medications, supplements and blood tests, yet each month the tests came back as being in the 'normal range'. I knew that what I was feeling wasn't normal, but I didn't know what was wrong with me. It took two years of living like this before I found a holistic doctor who diagnosed me with burnout, adrenal exhaustion and leaky gut syndrome.

It took another two years before my mental health and physical health stabilised. And I have spent a further ten years studying, researching, experimenting, learning and teaching both myself and others how to achieve both healthy and high performance.

Burnout is not an acceptable price for high performance.

Burnout is more than exhaustion

Many people describe themselves as 'burnt out' when they really mean 'exhausted'. So, let's take a moment to properly define it.

The World Health Organization classifies burnout as a syndrome 'resulting from chronic workplace stress that has not been successfully managed'.

There are three components to burnout:

1. **Energy depletion or exhaustion:** mental, emotional and physical

2. **Distancing or disconnection:** this may be mental disengagement, cynicism, lack of trust, negativity or possibly apathy

3. **Reduced performance or efficacy:** a loss of productivity and effectiveness (you are not getting things done in the way – or at the speed and quality – you usually would).

While burnout is not classified as a mental illness in and of itself, examples of health outcomes associated with burnout include depression, insomnia, type 2 diabetes, susceptibility to colds and cardiovascular diseases.

But burnout doesn't just negatively impact the health of the person experiencing it – it also adversely affects their ability to do their work and adds pressure to the rest of their team. Burnout outcomes at work include withdrawal behaviours such as absenteeism and turnover, decreased job performance, decreased job satisfaction, loss of engagement and commitment, and more interpersonal conflict with colleagues.

Solving burnout is a joint responsibility

While burnout has traditionally been viewed as an individual's problem to manage, the reality is that burnout won't be solved without leaders proactively managing for a healthy working environment.

Liam enjoyed the challenge of his job and became known as the go-to person for creative problem-solving of complex challenges for the team. He enjoyed being needed by the team, which boosted his self-confidence.

Over time he felt increasingly stressed and exhausted from the pressure of keeping up with his own work while providing the team with extra help.

Liam ignored the early signs of burnout and continued to push himself, not wanting to let others down. He began to develop other signs of burnout, including:

- physical symptoms: he experienced frequent headaches and muscle tension, and found himself getting sick more often and struggling to get a good night's sleep
- emotional symptoms: he felt emotionally drained and became irritable and impatient with his colleagues
- reduced productivity: his work began to suffer as he struggled to concentrate and found himself making mistakes
- lost motivation: he lost his positivity for problem-solving and enthusiasm for his work, and began to question if he was in the right job.

Liam realised he couldn't continue like this. He reluctantly spoke to his manager and shared his concerns about the workload and the toll it was taking on his mental and physical health.

His manager reassured him that he was a valuable part of the team. Together, they agreed on his core work priorities, agreed on a plan for how to better manage the team problem-solving requests as they came up and identified tasks that could be delegated to others.

To support his wellbeing, they agreed that he would start 30 minutes later each morning so he could attend a class at his gym, and they ensured that time was built into his schedule for a lunch break each day.

They scheduled a fortnightly check-in to see how this was working for him and make adjustments if needed.

How you communicate, prioritise work, provide autonomy, proactively manage workloads, support flexible working practices, and respect and model boundaries to working hours and wellbeing adds or detracts from a mentally healthy working environment.

Lily prided herself on being the top performer in her team – someone who could handle any challenge that came her way. But lately, she had been feeling overwhelmed and exhausted. The demands of her job seemed to be never-ending, and she felt like she was constantly playing catch-up.

The team had a micromanaging and demanding leader who often dumped requests on them with little notice. Lily had been shielding the team from the unreasonable requests coming their way by taking on more and more tasks herself.

Even though she didn't have the time or energy to do all these tasks, Lily was convinced that she was protecting the team from stress and burnout. But as her workload piled up, Lily found herself mentally drained, struggled to cope and became a bottleneck for team decisions.

THERE ARE BOTH WORK CAUSES AND PERSONAL CONTRIBUTORS TO BURNOUT

I invite you to read through these checklists and rate on a scale from 1 to 5 where you currently see yourself for each item. A rating of 1 represents a major problem for you, 3 is neutral and 5 represents a source of strength for you.

Let's start with the work causes of burnout:

1. **A mismatch between job demands and resources:** you experience excessive job demands without the training, resources or tools to successfully complete the work.

   Rating _____

2. **Excessive workload:** you experience regular overwork and excessive hours.

   Rating _____

3. **Lack of autonomy:** you lack control over the key decisions that affect how you do your work, or you don't have access to the people who need to provide you with information or guidance. This may also occur when you experience excessive micromanagement from others.

   Rating _____

4. **A purpose and values misalignment:** you don't feel a sense of integrity around what you are being asked to do; you are being asked to do things that are contrary to what the organisation stands for; or you don't feel that your role contributes to a meaningful, bigger picture.

   Rating _____

5. **Unhealthy working relationships:** you don't feel valued or like your efforts are recognised or matter. People aren't treated fairly – there is bias, favouritism or mistreatment tolerated by others.

Rating _____

There are also personal characteristics or lifestyle challenges that can make us more or less susceptible to burnout at an individual level:

1. **Worriers or ruminators** mentally run through different scenarios and courses of action with multiple contingencies for if things go wrong.

Rating _____

2. **Perfectionists** set unrealistic demands and expectations for themselves and are often described as having high standards or standards that are higher than are requested of them.

Rating _____

3. **Introversion** means you are the kind of person who derives energy from your own company, and you are overdoing extroversion practices at work such as group meetings and teamwork projects.

Rating _____

4. **Poor or out-of-balance health practices** means you have insufficient or inconsistent sleep, movement, nutrition, socialising, work-hours patterns and routines.

Rating _____

5. **Lacking trusting personal relationships** is when you don't have at least one close, trusting relationship at work and one close, trusting relationship outside of work where you can work through work-related problems and challenges.

   Rating _____

Note down your burnout sources of strength and your burnout areas of vulnerability.

_____

_____

_____

_____

_____

_____

_____

What do you need to address to reduce your susceptibility to burnout?

_____

_____

_____

_____

_____

_____

_____

OUR MENTAL HEALTH MAP

We fear and avoid what we don't understand. Facts and clear definitions matter.

At least one in five people each year are not okay, and half of those people are not accessing the professional help that could alleviate their suffering and support them to find a path for healing.

As leaders, it is important that we support people in having good mental health at work. This means providing a healthy environment and playing an active role in managing the work causes of stress and burnout before they get out of hand.

When we see someone struggling, we need to reach out and make the effort to connect. We don't need to know what their specific reasons are for struggling or not feeling safe enough to reach out for help; we just need to know that stigma and barriers exist – and be prepared to make the first move.

How many times have you said the following?

'If you need help with anything, just sing out.'

'If you need help with that project, just ask.'

'My door is always open if you need anything.'

Instead of putting the onus on your people to break through their fear and blocks, as a leader you need to proactively check in and offer the support they need.

LEADING WELLBEING TOOLKIT

Here are some tips for creating a healthy work environment:

- **Create a positive and inclusive work environment:** Encourage teamwork, idea sharing, the debate of multiple options, positive and constructive feedback, and offers of help.

- **Foster open communication:** Create rituals in meetings where people can discuss concerns and challenges and get help. Schedule regular individual check-ins to discuss workload, progress and any wellbeing issues.

- **Encourage breaks and boundaries:** Encourage the team to take breaks, set reasonable expectations for workload and deadlines, and provide support to prevent regular overwork.

- **Support social care and self-care:** Prioritise lunch breaks, support time for exercise, provide learning opportunities, be flexible with time for personal appointments and organise team social catch-ups.

- **Give recognition and rewards:** Express appreciation for individuals and the team on a regular basis. Acknowledge effort, experimentation, learning, helping out and progress. Celebrate achievements both large and small.

- **Provide support for mental health and wellbeing:** Build team mental health literacy, try out the EAP and share with your team how it helps, engage the team in wellbeing challenges that all can take part in, and support health messages and awareness campaigns.

CHAPTER 2

OUR ROLE

Sarah approached her leader Ben and asked if they could have a private conversation. Ben immediately felt anxiety build in his stomach. Sarah had been taking excessive sick leave and was missing deadlines, which he suspected was related to personal issues.

Sarah was usually one of his top performers and Ben didn't want to upset her by coming across as prying. But the team was asking questions about what was going on with Sarah and wanted to know how long they would need to shoulder the extra work created by her absences.

Sarah told Ben that she was caring for a family member who had been recently diagnosed with a chronic illness, and that she was struggling with worry for her family, the burden of care, poor sleep, a cold that she couldn't kick and the stress of letting the team down at work.

Ben froze with the fear of not knowing what would be an appropriate response.

Leaders have the potential to either transform someone's experience at work or traumatise them. The most common challenge leaders experience is finding the right balance between personal probing and professional care for a person's wellbeing at work.

Developing positive leadership skills helps you to help your people do their best work, be resilient under pressure and grow to their potential. It enhances a mentally healthy working environment.

But there is less clarity across most leadership styles when it comes to knowing how to appropriately support someone who is struggling.

The leaders I speak with are concerned by a lack of detail and understanding on what their role is and how to connect with a team member who may be experiencing mental health and wellbeing issues at work:

> *'If I ask someone about their mental health, wouldn't this be seen as prying into their personal life?'*

Many leaders don't feel equipped or confident to respond to mental health and wellbeing concerns:

> *'I am not an expert; if someone on my team shares that they are not okay or has a mental health issue, what should I say or do, or not say or do?'*

One of the greatest fears shared with me is that, if one of their team members shares that they aren't okay, it then becomes their responsibility:

> *'If one of my team shares that they aren't okay, doesn't it then become my job to fix it?'*

> *'Where will I find the time with my already overwhelming workload to give someone more support?'*

In the midst of our own uncertainty, we can avoid mental health check-in conversations because we feel ill-equipped with a lack of knowledge, skills or capacity – or all of these.

So, let's provide some clarity around what our leadership role is, and let's take some pressure off our worries by putting some healthy boundaries around what the leader role isn't.

WHAT OUR ROLE IS

When we notice a colleague struggling with mental health challenges, our role is to:

1. provide a safe and confidential space to share how they are feeling
2. encourage them to connect to relevant professional help
3. provide reasonable adjustments and appropriate support.

We need to accept at face value the truth of the person's experience as they see it and how they are experiencing it. We must be vigilant in not allowing our personal judgements to cloud our listening – our beliefs, values, thoughts and experiences maybe useful for us, but they are not relevant or helpful to them.

> Ben asked Sarah if she would like to go to the café down the road for a coffee away from the team. Sarah appreciated this consideration and told him about her problems at home and the toll it was having on her. She shared that she didn't know how long it would take for her to access professional carer support and that her doctor had diagnosed her with anxiety.

When someone shares with vulnerability and trust, it is important that we listen to what they say with empathy, confidentiality and respect for their autonomy.

> Sarah then burst into tears and admitted she felt bad about letting the team down but that she didn't want them to know about her personal situation or feel obligated to help her at work.

What our role isn't

Before we delve into the skill set for appropriately supporting someone who is mentally unwell, let's briefly cover what our role is not. It is not our role to:

1. judge a person, their reality or their situation
2. problem-solve, project what we would do onto them or give them solutions
3. try to fix them or manage their recovery plan
4. hold them accountable for their health actions.

If we find ourselves thinking or saying 'You should...' or 'Why don't you...' there is a good chance that we are overstepping.

> Ben thanked Sarah for her trust in sharing with him what was going on for her. He reassured her that she was a valued team member, and that it was normal to experience ups and downs in life. He resisted the urge to give her suggestions and asked her how he could best support her during this time at work.

Unlearning the impulse to solve is really hard

As human beings we find it very difficult to see someone in pain, because their distress can make us feel uncomfortable, upset, sad or distressed in return. Naturally, we want to make that pain go away as quickly as possible, both for them and for us.

As leaders, we learn very early on in our careers that the path to success includes anticipating problems, scenario-modelling, contingency-planning, problem-solving, and then quickly and efficiently fixing projects that have gone off course.

Many of us have also received feedback along these lines:

'Don't come to me with a problem; bring a solution.'

'There is no such thing as a problem, only an opportunity.'

'Come to me with your ideas, not just the problems.'

It is also difficult to resist going into solver mode when we can see actions a person can take that will help but they are resistant or aren't ready.

SKILLS FOR SUPPORTING SOMEONE WHO IS STRUGGLING AT WORK

So, let's now focus on the skill areas that are helpful for us to master when supporting our people's mental health and well-being. We will look at each of the following in turn:

1. providing a psychologically safe working environment
2. managing privacy and confidentiality
3. making reasonable adjustments
4. not discriminating.

Different states, territories, cultures and countries have different guidelines, policies and regulations when it comes to psychological safety, managing psychosocial hazards, making reasonable adjustments and discrimination, so the following are meant as guiding principles for your leadership toolkit. It is important that you familiarise yourself with any guidelines and policies applicable to your organisation and regulations that apply to your relevant geographical location.

PSYCHOLOGICAL SAFETY

Put simply, psychological safety is a shared belief held by all members of a team that the team is safe for interpersonal risk-taking.

In my twenties, I was promoted to my first senior leadership role, joining an executive team of very experienced, well-intentioned older males who had been working together for a number of years. In board meetings they would make a point of seeking my input – and then progressively dismiss my ideas due to reasons such as my younger age, not enough time in the role or not knowing one of their unwritten rules.

I stopped contributing to discussions unless they were on a topic that I cared passionately about and had overprepared a business case for. In my annual performance review with the CEO, I was told that I needed to learn to speak up.

As leaders, we have a responsibility to provide a psychologically safe environment for work in which all of our team members are able to contribute and do their best.

A lot has been written in the academic literature and in regulations, policies and procedures about what psychological safety is, but less on how to recognise when we do or don't have it with our own people. So, let's talk about what everyday psychological safety looks like.

Many organisational cultures have an unwritten decision-making default process that if the majority agrees with an idea or course of action, the team will proceed. We have expressions such as the following:

> 'Are you on or off the bus?'
>
> 'If you are off the bus, are you going to get on the bus or find another bus?'

Leading with psychological safety means creating a bus that everyone has a place on and wants to be on.

Bringing psychological safety to life

If you have a team of ten members and nine feel safe bringing their whole self to the group, but one team member doesn't, do you have psychological safety?

No. All ten need to feel safe to contribute to the best of their ability.

In a team meeting of eight people, if six are contributing and two are sitting back quietly, where does the onus sit for gathering input from all eight? On the two sitting back to speak up? On the six contributing to make space in the conversation for the two sitting back? On the leader for creating the environment and ground rules for sharing?

The leader needs to create the environment and ground rules for sharing and then support the team in actively including all voices. As leaders, to create psychological safety we may need to break some automatic habits and unhealthy patterns within our current group dynamics.

How many times have you sat in a meeting and asked for ideas with a ground rule of 'There is no such thing as a bad idea', but when someone volunteers something it gets shot down in flames or met with groans and eye rolls, or thrown out because 'We've done that before and it didn't work' or 'My guys won't do that'?

What if the two sitting back in our example don't feel comfortable or safe sharing their views in front of others? What if one of them has a history of being publicly ridiculed for an idea?

What if one of them has a history of being picked on because of their accent?

What are other ways, outside of making people speak up in front of everyone in meetings, that you could collect input so that all eight people can bring their best? Here are some examples of other ways to make sharing ideas feel safer:

- Invite input on key decisions prior to the meeting.

- Ask for ideas in your scheduled individual one-on-one meetings.

- Invite people in the meeting to discuss their ideas in pairs or small groups and then nominate a person to share their input with the larger group.

Encouraging difference and debate

Psychological safety doesn't mean creating a completely comfortable environment of consensus. Encouraging differences, diversity and multiple perspectives is fundamental for growth and learning.

Psychological safety in action means nothing you say or do will be used against you as long as you mean well, and your teammates will assume you mean well unless proven otherwise. Speaking up with a point of view that is different or uncomfortable is received with curiosity and discussion by a group. It helps expand the group's thinking, options, innovation and problem-solving.

Shutting down someone's ideas or information cuts off connection and communication, and reduces psychological safety and team progress.

Making it okay to not be okay

Providing psychological safety means that the people in your team know that it is okay to not be okay. They can safely share when they don't know something, ask questions when they don't understand, share when they notice something is wrong, and make mistakes and know it won't be held against them.

Importantly, psychological safety means an environment of trust. This means that when people are struggling with stress, burnout or mental health problems, they can share what is going on for them and be able to access support, knowing that people will be open and happy to help, and not get cranky about it.

How do we know when we have psychological safety?

We know we have a psychologically safe team when descriptors such as those in Table 1 are used.

Table 1: Descriptors when psychological safety is present

accepting	appreciative	clear
cohesive	connected	constructive
empowering	engaging	fair
flexible	friendly	inclusive
just	listened to	motivating
open	positive	respectful
rewarding	safe	straightforward
supportive	tolerant	trusting
valued	welcoming	worthwhile

We know we have work to do on psychological safety with our team if descriptors such as those in Table 2 are used.

Table 2: Descriptors when psychological safety is absent

aggressive	combative	confusing
discriminatory	disrespectful	draining
exclusionary	exhausting	ignored
inconsistent	isolating	micromanaging
negative	over-controlling	overwhelming
stigmatising	stressful	tense
tough	toxic	uncaring
unfair	unmanageable	unrealistic
unsafe	unsupportive	valueless

The good news is that investing in building psychological safety also brings a range of performance benefits. Research shows that psychological safety encourages open and authentic interpersonal behaviours, increases job engagement and satisfaction, supports coping with pressure and stress on the job, and creates a supportive and inclusive team climate. These are all key elements that contribute to teams' healthy high performance.

PRIVACY AND CONFIDENTIALITY

People do not have an obligation to disclose their mental health challenges or mental illnesses unless there is a specific company requirement to do so, usually based on safety. So, first and foremost as leaders, it is up to us to create a psychologically safe and trusting environment in which our people feel safe enough to reach out to us when they need help.

If a team member gives us the privilege of their trust and chooses to share their mental health concerns with us, we have a foundational responsibility to maintain their privacy and confidentiality. This means not sharing their information with anyone else – including HR, their line manager or colleagues – without their permission.

It is important that you have a direct and collaborative conversation with the person about what level of confidentiality they need, who may or may not be brought into the communication loop and what that means in regard to the support you can provide. More people knowing can mean higher interpersonal risk felt by the person experiencing mental health problems, but it also means more opportunities for help and support.

A person may elect for complete confidentiality. As a general principle, if there is no risk to safety or breaching of company policies, it is important to respect and support their decision.

If you are concerned for their safety at work or the safety of their co-workers, or if a well-communicated company regulation has been breached, it is appropriate to share with others on a need-to-know basis with the intent of keeping the person, their colleagues and the company safe. An example of this is if someone is taking medication that is making them drowsy and their role involves driving vehicles or operating heavy equipment, and you are concerned for their safety and the safety of others in their vicinity, then you need to access help from HR. Another example is if your company has a well-publicised zero-tolerance policy for certain substances, and you have reason to believe that someone is affected by alcohol or drugs on the job, then you need to follow the company regulations and processes.

MAKE REASONABLE ADJUSTMENTS

Just as we would support someone recovering from a broken arm or managing a diagnosis of cancer with reasonable adjustments, we have a duty to support our team members experiencing mental health problems or mental illness with reasonable adjustments.

Most people will be able to continue to participate in and perform at work with a little flexibility. Often this flexibility is to allow them to attend professional appointments, or constitutes changes to work hours or schedules to enable them to contribute to the best of their ability. Providing flexibility also includes adjustments such as giving extra time for tasks, making changes to communication, offering more regular feedback and providing extra help.

Often our default position when someone discloses mental health problems is to offer time off to seek help. I encourage you to start by asking what flexibility they need rather than suggesting a block of time off from work. Research shows that the longer a person with a mental illness remains on sick leave, the less likely they are to return to work. In particular, anxiety may lead to the avoidance of situations that people find stressful, which in the longer term can exacerbate their anxiety.

Social support is also a key preventative factor for mental illness, and social connection and a sense of purpose and regular achievement all contribute to a person's wellbeing. These are all factors that can be provided by well-supported work.

This is not to say that if a person requests time off we don't support that request, but we should offer check-in points during their leave so that they can stay connected to their leader, their team and their work if appropriate.

DO NOT DISCRIMINATE

Just as you would not provide performance management rectification for someone who is underperforming without providing the support, resources, training and coaching for them to improve, it is important that you do not discriminate against someone struggling with mental health problems.

Discrimination may look like:

- threatening someone's job security with performance issues
- not providing them with opportunities to apply for interesting work, projects or promotions they would otherwise be considered for
- taking work off them or demoting them.

It is also important to be wary of inadvertently discriminating against someone through the best of intentions. We may think that we are being supportive when we proactively reallocate work, delegate their work tasks to others or provide more oversight or checks for their work, but we may be causing more harm than help. What if the work we reallocate is not a source of stress but something they are good at, enjoy and derive confidence from? What if delegating tasks to their colleagues sparks gossip or feels to them like a loss of status? What if extra checking of their work is experienced as micromanagement rather than support?

The best way we can help one of our team who is struggling with mental health problems is to ask them what reasonable adjustments and support they need. Start with their ideas, ask what their health professionals suggest and agree on the way forward together.

LEADERSHIP ROLE CHECKLIST

While there is no one-size-fits-all set of policies, guidelines or regulations, there are some guiding principles that will support leaders to appropriately check in and support, rather than assume responsibility for, someone experiencing mental health challenges (see Table 3).

Table 3: Defining our leadership role

Our role is	Our role is not
To notice the signs when someone isn't travelling well and check in.	To problem-solve or fix, or to take over or assume responsibility for their recovery.
To provide psychological safety so everyone on our team feels accepted and able to bring their whole self to work and take interpersonal risks.	To ensure team members conform to group preferences and comfort norms.
To provide privacy and confidentiality to support team members who may be struggling to reach out and ask for help, and to encourage them to access appropriate professional supports.	To share someone's mental health issues with others without their permission.

Our role is	Our role is not
To provide reasonable adjustments to support their participation and performance at work to the best of their ability.	To diagnose or judge what a person does or doesn't need, or can or can't do.
To ensure people aren't discriminated against.	To make unilateral changes to a person's tasks, workload or role, or threaten their job security.

LEADING WELLBEING TOOLKIT

Our work environment impacts mental health both positively and negatively.

Work is an important source of wellbeing. It provides purpose and meaning, social connection and belonging, financial security and personal growth.

Bringing out the positive elements of work enhances both mental health and performance. Examples include:

- nurturing team psychological safety
- educating people on how to talk about mental health in a compassionate and supportive way
- fostering strong working relationships
- adopting a positive leadership style
- taking a strengths-based approach to developing people
- providing regular constructive feedback
- rewarding positive behaviours
- co-designing and crafting work
- providing regular opportunities for personal and professional development.

Work can also negatively impact mental health. Experiences such as unreasonable demands, under-resourcing, micromanagement, bullying or harassment can harm mental health, confidence and performance. People can also be negatively impacted by outdated leadership practices, poorly handled change, poor work design or the lack of organisational policies, technology or management processes.

Minimising the negative elements of work reduces mental health risk. Examples include:

- ensuring people have safe ways of raising concerns at work without negative consequences
- introducing planning, processes and consultation for how to manage periods of increased demands, pressure, disruption or change
- providing effective training in mental health and wellbeing literacy across the organisation for leaders and supervisors
- educating people in how to recognise the signs of stress, burnout and mental health problems, and how to access support
- complying with the legal obligations for your jurisdiction relating to work health and safety, workers compensation, workplace relations, privacy and discrimination
- taking proactive and systematic approaches to address bullying, harassment and discrimination
- implementing preventative psychosocial hazard identification and management.

CHAPTER 3

SEE THE SIGNS

Unlike physical injury or illness, the signs of mental illness are not immediately visible. When you look at the pleasant smiling face of the man in Figure 3, would you be able to detect the anxiety that he is feeling?

Figure 3: Hidden anxiety

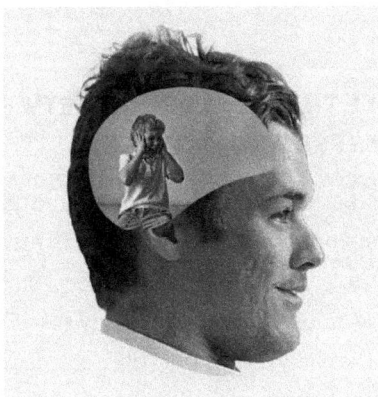

Often a smiling face on the outside masks a myriad of experiences, wounds, stories and suffering on the inside that we don't know anything about. Fear – especially fear of stigma – means that people are likely to mask or hide how they are really feeling, especially at work.

There is no one way that mental health manifests. Every person is unique in how they present themselves. So, what we are looking out for are changes to what is 'normal' for that person. When we use the term 'normal' in a wellbeing context, what we are talking about is how that individual usually shows up, reacts, interacts and behaves.

So, if someone who is usually chatty and social when they are in the office starts avoiding coffee and lunch catch-ups with colleagues, that signifies a change to how they would normally interact. But if another colleague prefers to take their breaks on their own to read or listen to a podcast and chooses not to socialise with their colleagues at lunch, them doing this wouldn't be considered a change to their preferences and how they would usually interact.

HOW DO I TELL THE DIFFERENCE BETWEEN EVERYDAY STRESS AND DISTRESS?

It is natural to experience ups and downs and periods of stress. For example, someone may shift down their mental health continuum for a couple of weeks because they feel really stressed out when moving house or starting a new job. This stress is not a sign of clinical anxiety but a one-off, reasonable reaction to a high-pressure situation that they are facing. Usually, the stress will resolve itself when the situation has been resolved, and they will recalibrate towards wellbeing.

A situation becomes a mental health problem when a person's feelings are of such high intensity and long duration that they start to impact the person's ability to function in everyday life and perform their normal activities.

Jordan had been working in the team for three years. He had always been a solid performer at work, and his colleagues valued him for his reliability and attention to detail. Over the last few months, he had been struggling with his mental health.

Jordan was finding it increasingly difficult to control his emotions. He would often get angry and irritable with his colleagues and would snap at them for no apparent reason. On other days, he could be overly emotional and find himself close to tears at the slightest provocation. Some afternoons he needed to leave work early because of headaches and brain fog.

Jordan was also struggling to meet deadlines and making mistakes that he wouldn't usually make. His colleagues noticed that he was becoming increasingly disorganised and forgetful, and his work was suffering as a result.

As leaders, we are not trained to diagnose, but we have three areas where we can look for changes to help us to identify when someone may be experiencing more than everyday stress:

1. Changes in emotional intensity
2. Duration of the changes
3. Adverse impact on functioning.

CHANGES IN EMOTIONAL INTENSITY

Changes in emotional intensity may be high or elevated, or low or underreacting.

High intensity might look like an overreaction in relation to what would be someone's usual response to a situation. We might see tears, anger, snapping, aggressiveness or defensiveness in response to something that wouldn't usually provoke much of a reaction.

At the other end of the scale, we may notice an underreaction to someone's usual response to a situation. We might notice apathy, withdrawal, an absence or uncharacteristic agreeableness in response to an issue or situation that a person would usually care about and invest time and energy in.

DURATION OF THE CHANGES

A person's change in reactions or behaviours needs to last longer than an off day, or a stressful week, or a few weeks of struggling with bad news, or a few months of working their way through a natural process of grief. There needs to be longevity to the change, where the changes we notice become a new pattern of behaviour for the person.

ADVERSE IMPACT ON FUNCTIONING

We also start to see a deterioration in a person's ability to function in everyday life and perform their normal activities.

A drop in in everyday functioning might look like reduced participation in regular hobbies or sporting activities that they would usually participate in outside of work – things like missing book club catch-ups, not turning up for soccer games and then dropping out of the team, not taking the dog for a regular morning walk, missing social events or declining social engagements you know they would usually enjoy.

A deterioration in performance might look like a loss of productivity. Tasks take them longer than they usually would. They may be slower in processing information or making decisions. They may struggle to remember information and lack their usual confidence in completing tasks. Or we might see a reduced quality of work from them – work that is incomplete, less detailed or containing more errors than usual.

THE SIGNS ARE OBVIOUS WHEN YOU LOOK FOR THEM

There are a myriad of observable signs that help us recognise when someone isn't travelling well, as well as a number of small signs that indicate poor wellbeing. One way you can start to identify potential mental health challenges in other people is by being aware of how stress and poor mental health shows up in yourself.

The signs for poor mental health can be physical, emotional, behavioural or relating to productivity. Physical signs may include the following:

- **Personal hygiene changes:** dishevelled appearance or more attention to appearance
- **Physical complaints:** headaches, aches and pains, gastrointestinal problems
- **Cognitive changes:** difficulty concentrating, focusing or with memory

- **Differences in sleep patterns:** not being able to sleep or sleeping all the time
- **Changes in weight:** losing weight or putting on weight
- **Movement changes:** moving more slowly or more rapidly
- **Greater substance use:** tobacco, alcohol or drugs.

Sometimes the physical signs may be what we notice first. Particularly when people have experienced long periods of stress or are tired, exhausted or burning out, we may notice an increased susceptibility to colds or illness before we think to check in on their mental health.

Emotional signs may include the following:

- **Emotional distress:** crying, complaining
- **Emotional extremes:** excessive fear, rumination or worry
- **Withdrawal:** apathy, isolating from others, reduced participation
- **Negativity:** excessive criticism, complaining, sarcasm
- **Conflict:** unusual troubles with colleagues.

Behavioural signs and productivity changes may include:

- erratic behaviour
- attendance changes, such as more frequent absenteeism, increased lateness or earlier leaving
- reduced productivity – less work produced, work tasks taking longer or problems with timeliness of delivery
- reduction in performance – deteriorating quality of work, errors in work or accidents
- reduced engagement and effort

- loss of confidence
- indecisiveness
- difficulty with information retention, prioritisation or time management
- reduced participation in work activities.

Leaders who identify these warning signs will be in a better position to provide support to people who may be struggling or in distress.

We don't need to know why someone is showing signs. The same signs may appear if a person is experiencing anxiety, having marital difficulties or struggling with caring responsibilities. We just need to recognise when an individual is experiencing some kind of struggle or crisis and check in based on the observed behaviours rather than trying to speculate, hypothesise or attempt to find out a cause.

We don't need to know what is going on with someone to recognise when they could benefit from a check-in and support.

SEE THE SIGNS CHECKLIST

Research shows that early support for someone exhibiting signs of stress, distress or struggling to cope improves their health outcomes.

There will usually be a number of small physical, emotional and behavioural clues that either ourselves or someone we know maybe struggling with their mental health and wellbeing (see Table 4).

Table 4: See the signs checklist

Changes	Signs	What I have noticed
Physical differences	Appearance Energy Sleep Physical ailments Weight	
Emotional intensity	Distress Erratic Excessive mood swings Withdrawal Conflict	

Changes	Signs	What I have noticed
Behavioural pattern changes	Attendance Effort Quality Quantity Timeliness	
Period of time changes observed for	Day Week Weeks Month Months	

LEADING WELLBEING TOOLKIT

You and your colleague Charlie have been working virtually for the past year and recently started a new project together. Charlie is usually chatty, collaborative, outgoing and eager to plan social events, even if it is just online trivia for the team.

Over the past month you have noticed that Charlie seems less engaged and enthusiastic in offering opinions and organising events and is showing up to meetings with their camera off.

In weekly team meetings Charlie has seemed tired and irritable, and a few times has lost patience with team members. When you casually ask Charlie how they are doing over a phone call, they shrug you off, saying they just haven't been sleeping well.

When you check in with Charlie a few days later to discuss some timelines for the project, they are indecisive and lacking their usual initiative.

Reflection questions

What are the signs that show Charlie isn't doing so well and could benefit from a check-in conversation?

Physical

_____

_____

_____

_____

Emotional

_____

_____

_____

Behavioural

_____

_____

_____

What are the indicators that Charlie may be
experiencing mental health challenges?

Emotional intensity

_____

_____

_____

Duration of changes

_____

_____

_____

Adverse impact on functioning

_____

_____

_____

CHAPTER 4

SELF-ASSESSMENT

Sam was a finance manager who oversaw a team of ten people. Despite noticing that a few team members seemed stressed and burnt out, Sam was reluctant to address the issue of mental health and wellbeing with them. Sam believed that mental health was a personal issue for employees to manage for themselves and ignored it.

One day a couple of team members approached Sam together and expressed concern about the stress levels at work and how it was affecting their mental health. Sam was taken aback and didn't know how to respond.

Over the next couple of months, Sam continued to ignore the issue, and the team's stress levels continued to escalate. Team members stopped talking to Sam and started taking more time off work, and team performance declined.

Eventually Sam realised that the deterioration in team performance wasn't going to improve. They realised that their avoidance of the issue and reluctance to talk about mental health was contributing to the burnout and stress the team was experiencing. By avoiding the issue, they had created an environment in which team members didn't feel safe enough to communicate openly about what they needed.

WE LACK THE CONFIDENCE TO HELP

Many leaders that I speak with feel ill-equipped and ill-prepared to have mental health and wellbeing conversations. Their concerns usually fall into three areas:

1. **lack of competence:** knowledge and skills in mental health

2. **lack of capacity:** time, space, energy, or mental and emotional bandwidth

3. **lack of confidence:** the confidence or courage to have conversations that feel personally risky.

Yet mental health literacy is a necessary skill for supporting people and high performance at work. Research shows that the employees of people managers who support wellbeing feel more valued, supported, empowered and engaged.

WE NEED TO DEVELOP MENTAL HEALTH LITERACY

Mental health literacy is our ability to recognise the early signs of mental health problems, know appropriate mental health and wellbeing language, and have the confidence to initiate supportive conversations and provide help.

When we improve our understanding of mental health issues, we create more supportive and inclusive environments that reduce stigma and enable us to have better conversations. This enables us to identify and address stress and mental health issues early and promote wellbeing practices.

Developing our mental health literacy as leaders at work has three parts:

1. clarity and understanding of our role for creating psychological safety at work

2. knowledge and understanding of mental health issues and potential symptoms

3. communication, wellbeing and support skills.

MENTAL HEALTH MASTERY SELF-ASSESSMENT

To improve your mental health literacy, it helps to start with a self-assessment (or diagnostic) of your strengths and gaps. For each of the following statements, choose the rating that best matches your level of confidence for that competence. Then, tally up how many times you rated each confidence level and give yourself an overall score (see Table 5):

1. You would need HR help with that competence.

2. You are not confident.

3. You would be confident only if you knew the person well.

4. You are confident some of the time.

5. You are confident most of the time.

6. You are confident.

65

Table 5: Mental health mastery self-assessment

	1	2	3	4	5	6
I feel confident in providing the appropriate level of psychological safety for my team.						
I feel confident in normalising mental health issues and supporting everyday wellbeing practices with my team.						
I feel confident I am modelling psychological safety, wellbeing and healthy work practices.						
I feel confident I would recognise the signs that someone may be developing burnout or a mental health problem.						
I feel confident approaching someone who may be developing a mental health problem or experiencing a mental health crisis.						
I feel confident in starting a check-in conversation with someone whose mental health I have concerns about.						
I feel confident that I am providing the trust, rapport and psychological safety that my team members need to be able to approach me with their mental health concerns.						

	1	2	3	4	5	6
I feel confident that I demonstrate active listening to my team members and try to understand both personal and professional concerns as they arise.						
I feel confident in knowing how to respond to someone who discloses mental health issues to me at work.						
I feel confident I know my role and responsibilities in supporting a team member experiencing mental health problems.						
I feel confident in offering a person reasonable adjustments and support for their mental health challenges at work.						
I feel confident I have a range of resources to access and adapt for myself and my team for different mental health support needs.						
I feel confident I can appropriately manage both care and performance for someone with mental health issues.						
My overall confidence rating						

Mental health mastery personal development plan

Now list your top three mental health mastery strengths.

Leveraging your strengths is one of the best ways to develop the confidence to tackle aspects of conversations that you feel less comfortable with.

Note next to each of your strengths a couple of ideas for how you could use more of that strength.

1. _____

_____

_____

2. _____

_____

_____

3. _____

_____

_____

Here are some examples of how you might leverage strengths:

- If your team finds you easy to approach, how could you create more opportunities for informal conversations with them?

- If you have a regular health and wellbeing routine that you maintain under work pressure, how can you support your team to invest in members' self-care?

- If you have a strength in active listening, how can you show more appreciation for each of your team members' contributions?

- If you have a strength in talking openly about mental health and wellbeing, how could you normalise mental health and wellbeing conversations across the team?

Now choose up to three mental health mastery gaps that you would like to focus on improving.

Note next to each of your gaps if the focus of your learning will be competence (skills), capacity (bandwidth), confidence (courage) or a combination.

1. _____

_____

_____

2. _____

_____

_____

3. _____

_____

_____

Here are some examples of development actions:

- Not sure how to recognise the difference between stress and potential mental health issues? Book in for mental health foundations training.

- Not sure what your organisational policies and supports for mental health are? Make time to research what is available. Book a meeting with HR to ask questions on anything you aren't sure of.

- Have you recognised the signs that one of your team members is struggling but are worried about how to approach them with your concerns? Make time with a confidential colleague and practise role-playing what you would like to ask.

- Not sure how to respond to someone with mental health issues? Work through some conversation case studies and identify the responses that feel most natural for you to speak.

- Feeling too stressed, busy or exhausted to initiate a mental health check-in conversation with a team member who you know is struggling? Review your workload, reprioritise your task list and take steps to support your mental health if it has taken a hit. Then, schedule a later time in your calendar to speak to your team member.

COMMIT TO IMPROVE

We are all capable of having more connecting, caring and supportive conversations with our team members. So, let's now look at strategies for how you can improve your conversational competence, capacity and confidence.

Increase competence

Improving your competence in having mental health conversations requires education, skills practice and reflection. Let's go back to our story with Sam...

Sam decided to participate in mental health training and develop their understanding of mental health issues and how to support the team. Sam noticed that Lee was showing signs of prolonged stress and struggling to deliver work that was usually easy for them.

Sam approached Lee and expressed concern for their well-being. Lee was hesitant to open up at first, but Sam was able to use their training to create a safe and non-judgemental space in which Lee felt able to share their concerns.

Sam used their new mental health literacy skills to listen, ask Lee how they could help, and offer support and resources. Sam encouraged Lee to access support from their EAP and offered flexibility to attend appointments and self-care activities.

They organised a weekly check in, which enabled them to discuss which strategies and supports were helpful, make changes in a timely manner and support Lee's performance.

Here are some strategies to improve your competence:

- **Educate yourself:** Learn about mental health, common mental health challenges and the best practices for supporting individuals experiencing mental health challenges. This can help you feel more confident and informed when having conversations about mental health.

- **Start with the types of education that best resonate with your learning style:** These may include books, podcasts, evidence-based fact sheets from reputable websites, eLearning or instructor-led training courses.

- **Practise self-reflection:** Reflect on your own biases and beliefs about mental health, and work to challenge any stigmatising or negative attitudes you may hold. By cultivating self-awareness, you can improve your ability to have productive and helpful conversations about mental health.

- **Develop active listening skills:** Active listening for wellbeing involves paying attention to what the other person is saying, validating their experience, and responding in a supportive and non-judgemental way. Active listening also helps build the trust and rapport necessary for psychological safety.

- **Practise empathy:** Empathy involves understanding and validating the other person's experience and emotions. By practising empathy, you can create a safe and supportive environment that can help the other person feel heard and understood.

- **Seek out feedback:** Seek feedback from trusted sources, a mentor, HR, a colleague or a mental health professional to help you identify areas for improvement and build your confidence in having mental health conversations.

By developing your knowledge, skills and attitudes, you can become more effective and confident in supporting individuals experiencing mental health challenges.

What action will you take to increase your skills and competence in mental health conversations?

_____

_____

_____

_____

_____

_____

Improve capacity

Capacity relates to the maximum amount of work, information or activities that we can healthily handle or process. This includes our physical and mental ability to take on and manage tasks and responsibilities.

Pritika had become caught in a cycle of regular, excessive hours at work, neglecting her personal life and feeling increasingly overwhelmed. She had a couple of team members who she was concerned about but was too exhausted to summon the energy for a supportive conversation for someone else.

Pritika knew that she needed take care of her mental health and wellbeing but didn't have the bandwidth to know where to start. She called the EAP offered by her company and shared her concerns with a counsellor about her mental and physical exhaustion.

Together, they created a plan, which included boundaries for working hours and prioritised self-care activities such as exercise, healthy eating and spending time with loved ones. Gradually Pritika noticed positive changes in her mood and energy levels and felt more capable of checking in with her team members' mental health.

Here are some strategies for improving your capacity for mental health and wellbeing support:

- **Start with you:** Take care of your physical and mental health. Regular exercise, a healthy diet, mindfulness practices and meditation, and sufficient sleep can improve your mood, energy levels and overall sense of wellbeing. Make sure to prioritise self-care and take time for yourself each day. This has a positive impact on your capacity to support others by giving you improved personal resilience, greater emotional intelligence in self-regulation and better cognitive processing for problem-solving. At the first sign of the wobbles, put on your own oxygen mask first. It is hard to show up for others' wellbeing when we are struggling with our own exhaustion, burnout or mental health challenges:

- *Manage your energy:* Exhaustion and burnout can leave you feeling physically and emotionally drained, which can make it difficult to find the energy to support others. Take the rest, breaks and recharging time that you need to show up in good shape.

- *Support your own mental health:* It is challenging to be emotionally available when you are dealing with your own feelings of anxiety, depression or stress. It is important that you prioritise professional services and personal supports for yourself.

- *Maintain healthy boundaries:* Actively manage your priorities and workload to within your capacity rather than to your exhaustion edge.

- **Prioritise mental health within the team:** Recognise the importance of mental health conversations as the foundation for healthy high performance and make this a priority. This may mean scheduling time in meeting agendas in the early stages of creating this element of psychological safety for your team.

- **Lead psychological safety:** Share your vulnerability and allow your team to provide you with support when you need it.

What action will you take to increase your capacity for
mental health and wellbeing with your team?

_____

_____

_____

_____

_____

_____

_____

Increase confidence

Increasing your confidence in mental health conversations at
work involves a combination of deepening your competence,
growing capacity and practising.

Practice takes effort, dedication and perseverance, which for a
new skill often feels uncomfortable and hard to stay committed
to during the short-term pain. So, here are a few reasons why
committing to practice has an exponential payoff:

- As you progress and improve, you will feel a sense of
  accomplishment, which can boost your confidence.

- Learning new skills helps you become more aware of your
  strengths and weaknesses. Addressing areas that need
  development builds your confidence in those areas in turn.

- Trying something new can be challenging, but it also
  expands your comfort zone.

- By overcoming obstacles and finding solutions for skills you
  are learning to master, you will feel more confident in your
  ability to handle challenges.

- Learning a new skill improves your adaptability and flexibility with new experiences and new situations.

- As you experiment and explore new ideas, you'll feel more confident in your ability to think outside the box when faced with uncertainty.

Leading psychological safety for our team also requires us to become comfortable with uncertainty, discomfort and personal risk.

The first strategy I suggest for increasing your confidence is **role-playing**. Role-play practice with scenarios helps to prepare you for challenging conversations and builds confidence in your ability to respond effectively when someone shares something difficult with you. Role-play is helpful in working out your approach, how to ask someone how they are, how to respond when someone shares something personal and how to offer appropriate support. It provides a safe and supportive environment to practise new skills, scripts and behaviours without fear of judgement or consequences.

Role-playing can help you understand other people's perspectives and viewpoints. By stepping into someone else's shoes, you can develop empathy and gain a new perspective on a situation, which can help your skills in navigating social situations more effectively. It also provides you with an opportunity to practise active listening, empathy and assertiveness, which can help you feel more confident in your ability to express yourself effectively in real-life situations. Receiving feedback from others will help you identify which areas to focus on.

I find that many people dislike role-plays, but this is one of the best ways to master difficult conversations. Feedback from my mental health training groups is that trying out new conversation structures using your own words in a safe environment provides the most transformative learning.

The second strategy I suggest for increasing your confidence is **case studies**. Working through case studies provides you with an opportunity to apply theoretical knowledge to real-world situations. By working through case studies at your own pace, you can gain valuable experience and build your confidence in your ability to apply the frameworks that you have learned in a practical way. Case studies also require you to make decisions based on limited information and data, which will help you make better decisions on what to say when under pressure. They also provide you with an opportunity for feedback and self-reflection, where you can identify areas for improvement and build your confidence in those areas.

What practice action will you take to increase your confidence?

_____

_____

_____

_____

_____

_____

_____

_____

_____

_____

MENTAL HEALTH MASTERY ASSESSMENT AND PERSONAL DEVELOPMENT PLANNER

Increasing your confidence in mental health conversations at work involves a combination of developing your competence, growing capacity and practising.

Your starting point is a self-assessment of your strengths and gaps. Start with a focus on mastering two or three competence areas at a time.

Strengths to leverage: _____

_____

_____

_____

Gaps to develop: _____

_____

_____

_____

Overall rating: _____ Target rating: _____

Self-reflections: _____

_____

_____

_____

_____

Development goals: _____

_____

_____

_____

_____

Competence development action: _____

_____

_____

_____

_____

Capacity development action: _____

_____

_____

_____

_____

Confidence development action: _____

_____

_____

_____

_____

How I will review progress: _____

_____

_____

_____

_____

PART II

THE MENTAL
HEALTH
MASTERY
FRAMEWORK

IN PART I we covered mental health challenges at work, our leadership role in providing psychological safety, and the importance of noticing and leaning in to support struggling colleagues. We worked through a personal self-assessment, and you identified your strengths and gaps in the skills you need to develop to have better mental health and wellbeing conversations.

In Part II, I provide you with the Mental Health Mastery Framework to increase your competence and include tips for supporting your capacity.

The most common challenges leaders share with me are how to approach someone they are concerned about at work, how to start a mental health conversation, what to say in response to personal disclosure and how to help.

There are five steps to building your conversation competence (see Figure 4).

Figure 4: The Mental Health Mastery Framework

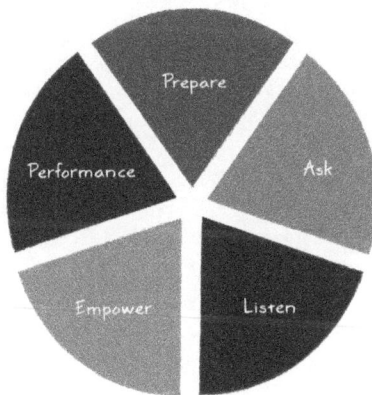

Use your self-assessment to choose which areas will be most useful for you to focus on first.

We will cover each step in turn:

1. **Prepare:** Plan your approach and what to say.

2. **Ask:** Start the conversation.

3. **Listen:** Show empathy and understanding.

4. **Empower:** Encourage action without taking on responsibility.

5. **Performance:** Balance care with performance conversations.

The Mental Health Mastery Framework provides you with strategies, structure and scripts to build your competence and capacity in having better conversations with your people.

It is then over to you to put it into practice!

CHAPTER 5

PREPARE

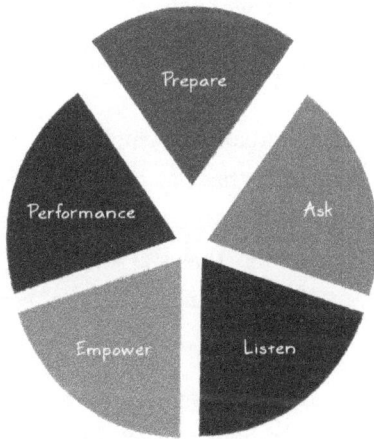

When you make a meal, there are some key preparation steps that you would never skip. You might create a list of ingredients, check the pantry and fridge to make sure that you have all the items you need, replenish anything that is missing and get out the equipment required. You then allow enough time to chop, cook, construct and serve an appropriate meal for the people and occasion you are providing for.

But many of us start an important conversation with someone we are concerned about with a blurted out, broad and generic question like 'Are you okay?' because we feel uncomfortable. Or we avoid saying anything at all because we don't know how to broach something personal. And not addressing the elephant in the room may lead us to avoid the person in general, exacerbating our discomfort but also isolating someone who may need help.

MAKE WELLBEING A NATURAL PART OF YOUR DAY

The more open, inclusive and everyday wellbeing conversations at work are, the easier it will be to approach a colleague when you are concerned about them.

Weekly team meeting rituals in which each team member is invited to share one thing that has gone well for them and one thing they need help with assists in building trust and vulnerability. One-on-one meetings that start with checking in on *how* someone is doing before moving onto *what* someone is doing builds connection and empathy.

You will naturally find some people easier to instigate a check-in conversation with and others harder, and that is okay. It will often be easier to recognise the signs and start a personal conversation with someone you know well, versus someone you see only a couple of times a week for a project. But with a little bit of preparation, you can bridge your comfort gap.

PREPARE FOR SUCCESS

By spending just 10 to 15 minutes preparing for a check-in conversation, you will boost your courage and confidence in how to approach someone appropriately at work. At the same time, you will be more likely to connect than disconnect with the person you are checking in with.

Let's work through each of the elements for preparation in turn:

1. Plan what you want to say.
2. Provide an invitation to speak.
3. Create a psychologically safe and comfortable environment.
4. Be present and generous with time.
5. Know your organisational policies and supports for mental health and wellbeing.

PLAN WHAT YOU WANT TO SAY

There will be a number of small signs, both physical and behavioural, that will have triggered your concern. What have you observed that is causing your concern? For example:

- They are tired and withdrawn when they are usually chatty and contributing to team discussions.

- They have stopped joining the team for social lunches when they are often an organiser of social lunches.

- They are missing deadlines when they usually pride themselves on punctuality.

- They are not contributing ideas in meetings on topics they usually care passionately about.

- They are asking for detailed feedback before finishing everyday tasks they would normally complete quickly and autonomously.

- They are catching more colds than usual during the flu season or when they take time off.

List the signs of change you have noticed in Table 6, along with how they differ to how the person would usually show up.

Table 6: Signs of change and usual patterns

Signs of change	Usual patterns

One of the things leaders often struggle with is how to transition from a task-oriented work conversation into the territory of a personal caring conversation. How do you move from talking about tasks, timelines, projects and deadlines to asking someone to share personal concerns and challenges without feeling clunky, awkward, confronting or inappropriate?

Having a selection of non-work-related, neutral and safe ice-breaker topic questions that you can ask will provide you with a clear way of signalling that the conversation is moving into personal interests.

With a colleague you know well, you may ask about topics such as:

- family
- hobbies
- weekend plans and activities
- holidays planned or holidays just taken
- house and DIY projects.

It is also helpful to talk about topics that you are also happy to share your own personal information and views on. Connection in conversations comes from mutual disclosure and sharing. For example, don't ask about their children if you don't want to talk about your children with them.

With an acquaintance or colleague that you don't know well, you may consider asking about:

- sporting interests and sports teams they follow
- favourite TV shows or TV series (reality TV, drama, crime, competitions)
- recent movies they have watched
- books or blogs they like to read
- music or podcasts they like to listen to.

Be prepared with a range of topics and views that you can also share. Some people will love sport and others will loathe sport. Some people will love cooking reality shows while others will prefer a crime series.

List your neutral icebreaker topics and your personal contributions:

_____

_____

_____

_____

_____

_____

_____

_____

PROVIDE AN INVITATION TO SPEAK

We have all had experiences of being hijacked at work and feeling worse off leaving the interaction. When a colleague catches you off-guard and bails you up in an open, public area, where other people can hear what is being said, to discuss a topic you feel unprepared for, it makes you feel unsafe, not safe. So, let's not do that!

Make your invitation light and informal, but also make it clear that you want to catch up on how they are doing, not what they are doing at work.

An in-person invitation can be as simple as this:

> 'Hey, it's lovely to see you. I realise we haven't chatted for a while. I'd like to catch up and see how you are. I have some time this later this afternoon or tomorrow morning; if one of those works for you, would you like to go for a walk down the street and grab a coffee together?'

If most of your communication with someone is via screens on a platform like Zoom or Teams, you can still create an invitation:

> 'Oh hey, I know this may sound a bit naff, but I've realised that most of our conversations are transactional and work-related – a downside of screen communication. Would you have time in the next couple of days for a virtual coffee catch-up? I haven't seen your smiling face on camera for a while and would like to check in and see how you are going. What time would work for you?'

If most of your communication with someone is on the phone, you can still create an informal check-in invitation.

'By the way, I have realised that so much of our conversation these days is work-oriented. I don't know about you, but I am spending too much time at my desk and missing social catch-ups. Would you be interested in a walk and talk? Let's find some time to put on our sneakers, you find a park near you, I'll find a park near me and let's catch up on how you are.'

CREATE A PSYCHOLOGICALLY SAFE AND COMFORTABLE ENVIRONMENT

If you want to encourage someone to open up about what is really going on for them, you need to create a safe, comfortable, private environment for them to share in.

If you are in the office, finding a meeting room might seem like the most logical choice. But if your meeting rooms are glass-walled and anyone walking past can see who is in there, or if the only time meeting rooms are used outside of team meetings is for performance discussions, a conversation in that space is more likely to escalate fear than provide safety.

If you are speaking with someone via screens, it is important not to assume that just because the person you are speaking with is the only person you can see in your view, they are alone. Often people working from home may have a partner next to them at the desk, or are supervising children's homework in the same room, or have pets demanding attention.

Here are some suggestions for informal places to talk:

- Grab a coffee out of the office.
- Have lunch together at a table for two in a quiet, private space outside of the busiest break-time hours.
- Head out for a walk and talk.
- Have a private Zoom or Teams chat.

When you meet, it is important to be clear at the outset that this is an informal and confidential conversation. You will find it helpful to set the context: it is an informal check in between colleagues, and anything discussed will be kept private and confidential.

It is important to be explicit that this is not a formal or documented discussion about the person or their performance, rather than assume that they know what a private conversation in a work setting means.

Use Table 7 to plan your psychologically safe and comfortable environment.

Table 7: Creating a psychologically safe and comfortable environment

Comfortable conversation location options	Psychological safety options

There will be instances in which you may not be able to keep the conversation completely private. If you are concerned for their immediate physical safety or about being able to keep them psychologically safe, you may need to involve someone to provide assistance. It is important that you are open, transparent and honest when the privacy context of your conversation changes.

If you find yourself in this position, collaborate with them on who would be the best person to involve – a support person outside of work, their doctor, a mental health first aider at work or someone from HR, or you could call the EAP or a helpline together.

BE PRESENT AND GENEROUS WITH TIME

Can you recall a time when you have been sharing something important in a conversation and been cut off by the other person? You are speaking to your parent and they pick up their phone when it rings. Or you are out at lunch with a friend, and a message notification pops up on their device and they start reading it? Or your manager at work has one ear on your conversation and one eye on the emails arriving in their inbox?

It doesn't feel good, does it?

Or when your over-busy manager says they have an open-door policy and you are welcome to pop in and speak to them at any time, but they are always on the phone, with someone, or in a meeting, is there really a genuine invitation there to speak?

What about when you finally get the time for your one-on-one meeting with your manager – the meeting that is two weeks overdue and has been rescheduled three times already – and your manager tells you when you start that you only have 20 minutes rather than the planned hour because they are double-booked.

Are you going to share what is really going on when faced with disinterest and disrespect?

An important part of providing psychological safety is demonstrating that you want to know how people are, that they are a valued member of your team, and that if something is troubling them you are there to listen and help. If a colleague at work gives you the privilege of their trust in sharing with you what is really going on for them and that they are struggling, you don't want to shut them down because you only have 15 minutes before your next meeting.

My rule of thumb is to allow an hour for a caring check-in conversation. If for some reason it only takes 15 minutes, then you have a bonus 45 minutes for a break or to knock something off your to-do-list. I don't know anyone that doesn't appreciate some extra time in their workday!

KNOW YOUR ORGANISATIONAL POLICIES AND SUPPORTS FOR MENTAL HEALTH AND WELLBEING

There is no one-size-fits-all approach when it comes to organisational policies for psychological safety and mental health. Some organisations have well-thought-through and documented policies and procedures; others don't have anything. There is an increased expectation from public regulators and in public policy that organisations are responsible for the psychological safety and wellbeing of their people, but this is still a developing area.

When you are preparing for a check-in conversation with someone you are concerned about, it helps to be literate in:

1. psychological safety guidelines
2. mental health policies and procedures

3. flexible work principles and policies

4. available supports for mental health issues, such as an EAP or access to medical professionals or counsellors

5. publicly available mental health and medical services and how to access them.

PREPARATION CHECKLIST

Taking 10 to 15 minutes to prepare for a check-in conversation will boost your ability to connect and increase the likelihood that the person you are concerned for experiences care rather than concern (see Table 8).

Table 8: Preparation checklist

What are the daily and weekly wellbeing check-in opportunities already in place?	Team meeting opportunities:
What conversation opportunity do you need to create?	One-on-one opportunities:
Plan what you will say. What have you noticed? How is that different to their usual?	Signs: Usual patterns:
What are some personal, neutral icebreaker topics you can connect with?	Icebreakers:

How can you create a comfortable, informal, private, safe space for a conversation?	Safe space:
What level of confidentiality can you give the conversation?	Psychological safety:
Prepare your mindset and time. Allow enough time.	Time:
Ensure you are prepared, able to be present and not being rushed.	Being present:
What are the relevant organisational policies and procedures? How is confidentiality managed?	Policies and procedures:
What supports are available? Who is available to help?	Mental health resources and supports:

PREPARATION TOP TIPS

By spending just 10 to 15 minutes preparing for a check-in conversation, you will boost your confidence and be more likely to connect than disconnect with the person you are checking in with.

1. List the signs and changes that you have noticed in the person.
2. Plan your opening questions and practise them out loud.
3. Give them a flexible invitation to catch up.
4. Plan for a private, comfortable place to speak and create psychological safety with confidentiality.
5. Be present and generous with your time, showing that you are genuinely interested and want to help.
6. Familiarise yourself with your organisational policies and supports for mental health and wellbeing.
7. Familiarise yourself with a couple of professional sources of support outside of the working environment.

CHAPTER 6

ASK

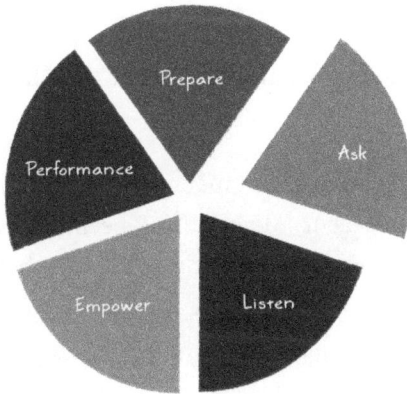

Many of the leaders I speak with hesitate to approach someone they are concerned about because they don't know how to start the conversation. What is holding them back?

Quite simply, it is fear. Fear of coming across as too nosy or too intrusive. Fear of offending the other person. Fear of saying the wrong thing and being misconstrued. Fear of coming across as professionally inappropriate. But the reality is, our fears are about the potential risk to our sense of self and our self-perception.

If we see someone struggling, it helps to focus our concern on them, rather than becoming overly caught up in the optics for ourselves. If you approach someone with care, psychological safety and a well-thought-out expression of concern, what is the worst thing they could say in response?

'Thank you for your concern, but I am fine.'

'Thank you for checking in, but I would prefer not to talk about personal matters at work.'

It's really not so scary, is it?

So, let's start leaning in, rather than leaning out.

Sophie was part of a customer service team and had noticed that her colleague Michael had been acting differently lately. He seemed constantly tired, his behaviour was erratic and he was struggling with client phone calls.

Sophie invited Michael to grab a coffee at a café down the road. On the walk there, Sophie asked Michael how his weekend parkruns were going. Michael shared that he was too tired for running.

After they ordered, Sophie asked Michael more about his tiredness. 'Michael, I have also noticed your tiredness and you seem to be a bit withdrawn lately. This isn't like your usual cheery self. I am concerned about you. How are you at the moment?'

Michael was initially hesitant to open up, but Sophie's caring approach made him feel more comfortable. He shared that he had been struggling with anxiety, having difficulties sleeping, and was struggling to think clearly and manage his workload. Sophie assured him that mental health challenges were common and that she was here to listen if he felt comfortable talking.

The perfect time to ask someone how they are is as soon as you notice any small signs that they may not be travelling so well. Don't create delays because you are waiting for the perfect opportunity, the perfect place, an in-person working day or better timing.

When in hybrid ways of working, pick up the phone and do a walk-and-talk, organise a virtual coffee over Teams or send a Skype message.

Create the best opportunity you can for a conversation that is informal and private as soon as possible:

'Hi Michael, we haven't caught up for a while; do you have time for a coffee today or tomorrow?'

HOW DO I START?

One of the biggest blocks people tell me they experience when instigating a check-in question is that they don't know how to start:

'How do I go from a work-related or task-related conversation to something personal without me feeling weird and them feeling uncomfortable?'

Abruptly changing course from talking about performance to asking personal questions is most likely going to land awkwardly. I find it helpful to use a neutral segue that provides a clear signal the conversation is transitioning. Starting with a non-work-related, neutral, open-ended icebreaker question sets the upcoming conversation context and encourages the person to open up and share their thoughts, views or experiences.

Start your questions with who, what, when, where, why or how.

With someone you know quite well, you might say something like this:

'How is your daughter going with netball?'

'What is your book club reading at the moment?'

'Where are you hiking/cycling/running next?'

With someone you don't know so well, you may prefer to pick something broader or a current event:

'What did you think about the game on Saturday night?'

'What did you think of the MasterChef elimination on Sunday night?'

Be direct

Many of us have grown up with the belief that being direct and personal is rude or inappropriate. This is not true. In fact, being direct and personal about your observations demonstrates that you have noticed, genuinely care and want to know how the person is.

This is quite different to how many of us have been brought up. We throw out general and generic greetings all the time and hope that they are sufficient.

When we ask, 'How are you?' we are not expecting anything other than a polite 'Fine, and how are you?' in return. 'How are you?' has turned into an extended version of 'Hello'.

We may get complicated and waffly when we feel uncomfortable:

'How are you? I mean, I have noticed you have been a bit withdrawn lately. But I am not implying that is a problem. If you don't want to answer you don't have to...'

And the person doesn't know how to answer, or gets lost in the question, and is more likely to answer with 'I'm fine'.

Language matters

If we are concerned about someone, we may ask, 'Are you okay?' or 'Is everything all right?' These are both examples of closed questions that can be shut down quickly without getting into difficult emotional territory. They can be answered with a one-word response and don't encourage the conversation to open up.

The other implication if we ask 'Are you okay?' is that we are signalling our preferred judgement or response, which is a reassuring answer like 'I'm fine', 'I'm good' or 'I'm okay, just busy'.

So, we need to be considered and direct with our check-in questions:

'I have noticed that you seem tired lately. This isn't like your usual bubbly self. I am concerned about you. How are things with you at the moment?'

Use 'I' statements

'I' statements project concern and care and increase connection. 'You' and 'we' statements can feel like an attack, even when they are not meant to be.

'I have noticed you are looking tired' projects empathy. 'You are looking tired' can feel like an accusation or invoke a need to defend. 'We have noticed you are looking tired' can provoke concern or worry. Who is we? What are people saying about me? Who is talking about me behind my back?

Get personal

What is it that you have noticed about the other person that is causing you concern? And how does it differ to how you would usually experience them?

> *'I have noticed that you seem tired lately. This isn't like your usual bubbly self.'*

> *'I have missed your smiling face at our weekly team lunches. It isn't like you to miss our social catch-ups.'*

> *'I have noticed that you have been quiet in our team meetings. I have missed your thoughtful contributions.'*

WHAT TO SAY AND WHAT NOT TO SAY

When someone isn't travelling so well, there will usually be a lot of small physical, emotional and behavioural signs that show up.

Set up psychological safety

It helps to list all the signs you notice in your preparation because, particularly in a workplace context, it is important to open with an observation that demonstrates you are concerned about their wellbeing – rather than a behavioural change, which may make them feel as though their performance is under attack. 'I have noticed that you are experiencing a lot of headaches' shows more concern for the person than 'I've noticed that you have been making a lot of mistakes and missing deadlines lately'.

Plan your check-in question

There are four phrases I find useful to start with in creating a considerate check-in question that shows care and also encourages someone to share how they are:

1. 'I have noticed...'

2. 'This is different to your usual...'

3. 'I am concerned...'

4. 'How are things going with you?' or 'How are you travelling at the moment?'

Practise out loud what you will say

It is important that you write down in your own words what you would say and then practise them out loud. Rearrange the structure as needed to sound natural and comfortable for the way you would usually speak:

'I have noticed that you aren't your usual bubbly self and seem increasingly tired. I am concerned about you. How are things with you?'

'I am worried that there may be something on your mind; you seem a little distracted in meetings. You usually thrive in team conversations. I would like to help. Please share what is going on for you.'

Pause and pace

We are asking quite personal questions, and so we need to give the person we are speaking to time to work out how they would like to answer.

If we rush them because we are feeling anxious, we may make them feel pressured. As human beings, we mirror each other, and our obvious discomfort may discomfort them and close down the conversation. Or if we are pushing them towards a solution or to take action, we may come across as disinterested or lacking understanding.

Encourage conversation with clarification questions

If someone places their trust in you and tells you what is going on in their world, show them that their vulnerability is welcome. Encourage them to keep sharing. If someone responds to you and shares that they have been feeling unusually tired, keep asking questions. Ask if they are dealing with anything out of the ordinary that might be contributing to their state.

Asking clarification questions supports them in opening up, and also provides you with more context for supporting their challenges:

> 'When you say you haven't been sleeping, how long has this been going on for? Do you have strategies to help you sleep?'

> 'With your family caring duties, do you have family or friends who are able to help?'

> 'When you say that you are feeling overwhelmed with your workload, what is worrying you the most?'

Often just talking it through and sharing their challenges can be a source of relief and wellbeing support. One of the kindest things we can do to support someone going through a tough time is to be a safe ear that listens.

WHAT IF THEY DON'T WANT TO TALK?

If someone doesn't want to talk or they aren't willing to admit that there's something going on for them, we need to respect their autonomy and wishes. It is not our place to force discussion of an issue that they are not ready, willing or able to discuss.

But we should give a respectful response that provides a message of care and encourages them to reach out for help:

'If I am not the right person for you to talk to, please speak to someone you feel comfortable with, as I am concerned about you.'

'I appreciate that you may not want to speak to me about this, but I do encourage you to reach out and speak to someone you trust, because I am concerned about you and care about your wellbeing.'

'I understand that this is not something you want to talk about at work, but I am concerned about you and encourage you to reach out to someone you trust outside of work to get some support.'

'I just want you to know that I am concerned about you and appreciate that there may be things you don't want to talk about at work. Our EAP is anonymous and free, and can provide guidance and support.'

'I am concerned about you, and if you do want to talk at any time, I am here. Would it be alright if I check back in with you next week?'

ASK CHECKLIST

Prepare, plan and practise your questions using Table 9.

Table 9: Ask checklist

Invitation to meet: • Coffee? • Walk?	
Neutral, open-ended icebreaker questions: • Sport • TV or movies • Music or podcasts	
Specific and direct check-in questions: • 'I have noticed...' • 'I am concerned...'	
Encouragement through clarification: 'Tell me more about what that is like for you...'	

ASK TOP TIPS

One of the biggest blocks to checking in with someone who is struggling is not knowing how to start and what is appropriate to say. This is where a little bit of preparation can provide a big payoff.

1. Begin with a neutral, open-ended question that clearly shows the conversation is not about how they are going at work but how they are as a person.

2. Be direct with your check-in question. Share what you have observed and how it differs to how they would usually show up. This shows you have noticed and care.

3. Using 'I' statements shows concern, whereas framing your questions with 'you' or 'we' can provoke defensiveness.

4. Be clear that the conversation is confidential, informal and not a performance discussion. This provides psychological safety and encourages sharing.

5. If the person doesn't want to share what is going on, it is their right not to speak. Be encouraging rather than judgemental and let them know you are willing to listen if they change their mind at any time.

CHAPTER 7

LISTEN

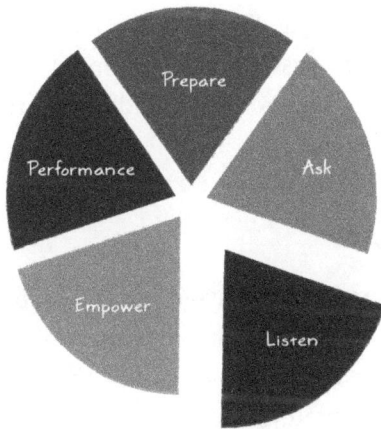

We aren't good at listening. There are studies showing that most people spend more time talking than listening.

The average person speaks at somewhere between 150 and 225 words per minute, but we can listen at up to 500 words per minute. So if we aren't actively focusing, our minds left to their own devices are busily filling in those extra 275-plus words with our own ideas and judgements on what the other person is saying.

Then, to round out the picture of our listening in conversations, the average person only remembers about 25% to 50% of what is said in a conversation.

Instead of hearing them, we are actually listening to ourselves.

It is more rewarding to talk than to listen. When you are talking, you are in control of the conversation. You can direct it towards the things that you want to hear about and away from topics that you aren't interested in.

So, we need to develop the ability to be fully present in the conversations we are having. We need to notice when our thoughts arrive and let them pass through our mind without becoming enmeshed in them. This is where mindfulness training and meditation practice helps.

WHAT DO I SAY?

One of the reasons why we avoid uncomfortable conversations is that when someone shares something really tough with us, we worry about what to say. We worry that if someone shares something that is upsetting for them, we won't know what to say because we are not qualified to have those conversations.

But the reality is that we need to stop focusing so much on saying and do more listening. And when we listen to empathise and not to solve, it takes the pressure off us to respond and enables us to connect more honestly and authentically.

We are now going to cover some of the strategies that will improve our listening:

- Listen to understand, not to solve.
- Empathise and validate feelings.

- Normalise their experience.
- Avoid judgement.
- Don't interrupt.
- Don't jump in with suggestions and solutions.

LISTEN TO UNDERSTAND, NOT TO SOLVE

Good listening involves approaching the conversation with curiosity and unconditional positive regard. I like to adopt this listening mantra:

**Everyone knows something that you don't –
prepare to be amazed.**

One of the challenges with listening in a work context is that we are usually listening to solve, or listening in order to gain just enough information to then be able to respond.

Most of us learn that to be successful at work, 'There's no such thing as a problem, only an opportunity'. Or we are told, 'Don't come to me with a problem; come to me with a solution'. And we take these frames with us into our mental health and wellbeing conversations.

This is when we need to select the off switch for those work-oriented productive listening habits.

We need to listen to understand. Empathetic listening can be as simple as saying, 'I am so pleased you told me; how can I help?'

Jack and Alicia were supervisors and colleagues at a large warehouse and distribution centre. Jack had noticed Alicia had been coming into work late, was forgetting tasks on shift and was often distracted.

One afternoon, Alicia asked Jack if she could speak to him confidentially. Jack found a quiet place for them to talk away from prying eyes and gave Alicia his full attention. Alicia shared that she was struggling with anxiety and depression, and it was impacting her work and personal life.

Jack listened attentively as Alicia shared her thoughts and feelings. He acknowledged her difficulties and responded with empathy, saying things like, 'I'm sorry to hear that you're going through this,' and 'It sounds like you're having a really tough time'.

Jack also asked open-ended questions to understand more, such as, 'How long have you been dealing with these feelings?' As Alicia opened up more, Jack responded with reassurance, telling her that what she was feeling was common, that she was not alone and he was there to support her.

Alicia felt heard and understood, and grateful for Jack's open-mindedness and kindness.

EMPATHISE AND VALIDATE FEELINGS

Many leaders feel uncomfortable demonstrating empathy at work because they worry that showing an interest in a person's distress means that they are agreeing with or endorsing something that they don't personally believe in. Or they worry that showing an interest in a person's struggles means they will assume responsibility for solving it.

This is not the case.

The most important part of listening well is to acknowledge and validate that what the other person is feeling is real for them. When we demonstrate empathy, we are showing that we are willing to listen and want to understand their perspective:

'I can appreciate that this is upsetting for you. I would like to understand more if you are willing to share.'

We also listen to increase our understanding of what they are experiencing, so paraphrasing back to them what we have heard is helpful for us and supports them in feeling heard:

'What I'm hearing is that your caring responsibilities at home are overwhelming and you are upset by the lack of support; am I understanding that right?'

NORMALISE THEIR EXPERIENCE

It is perfectly normal to experience ups and downs in life, and when facing tough times it is only natural to feel wobbly and need extra support. As leaders, a core element of psychological safety is to reduce the fear of stigma by demonstrating that it is okay to not be okay:

'Thank you for sharing your challenges with me. It is normal to struggle with feelings of overwhelm, and I am here to help.'

Even when we don't have experience with what the person is struggling with, we can still show up naturally:

'While I can't appreciate the process that you've been through, I can see that this is really distressing for you. Tell me more about what's going on for you.'

AVOID JUDGEMENT

When someone feels judged, they are less likely to open up and share what is really going on. When we show judgement, we are less likely to get the information we need to provide the best support we can.

So, avoiding judgement is important. It can also be difficult to do. As human beings, we are meaning-making judging machines. Everything we see, taste, hear, touch, smell, encounter or feel has a thought, belief, view or value applied to it by our brains. It happens automatically.

While we can't necessarily turn our judgement off, we can recognise when the meaning we are attributing to something is useful or not. We can choose to put our unhelpful views about someone's situation down, or to one side, with the intention of being fully present to what they are sharing in that moment.

Even if you don't agree with the content that is shared, you can still choose to let go of judgement and show empathy:

'I can see this is upsetting for you. I appreciate your courage in sharing this with me. Please tell me more about what is going on for you.'

'I appreciate how much you have been going through these last few weeks. How can we support you?'

'I can see this is distressing for you. I don't have experience of this personally; what can I do to help?'

DON'T INTERRUPT

One of the most valuable and caring things that we can do is simply listen and acknowledge the other person's experience.

When we ask a thoughtful, personal question, we need to give the person time to think it through and choose how they would like to respond. Many of us are uncomfortable with silence, and if we don't get a response immediately we may jump back in again with another question, suggestion or solution. Don't do that.

Be generous with pauses and be gracious with silence.

Sharing your experience disconnects

Many of us have been taught that if someone shares with us something personally tough, if we have a similar experience and share it with them then it shows we understand, and it builds rapport and trust. This is not true.

As soon as I start talking about my experience, I make the conversation about me instead of it being a conversation about you. No matter how well-meaning I may be, I am shutting you down.

No two experiences are ever the same

If someone shares with you their struggles caring for a critically ill family member, don't talk about the time you almost lost a loved one.

When we talk about our own experience, we are also sharing our meaning-making and judgements about it, and we are influencing what the other person thinks they should be feeling and thinking. We may make them feel judged or inadequate about the feelings that they are having. Let's not do that.

For example, if you felt flat, and they are feeling frightened, you are prompting them to review and evaluate the experience they are having against your emotional criteria, which is not relevant or useful to them.

When we insert our experience and what we did with that experience into the conversation, we're either shutting down the person or even potentially changing their experience.

If you would like to introduce into a conversation that you have experience with the view to show empathy and understanding, it is important that you ensure the focus begins and remains with the person you are supporting:

> *'I understand that this is a really tough time for you. I have some experience with depression in my family, which I would be willing to share with you at some stage if that would be useful. Tell me more about what this is like for you.'*

> *'I understand this is an upsetting time for you. I have experience with mental illness in my family. Would sharing some of my experience be helpful for you at some stage? What can I do to help?'*

You are providing the person with an open-ended invitation to ask you questions, without an expectation that they need to listen to your story:

> *'I understand this is a really tough time for you. I have some experience with depression with my family. Would sharing some of my experience at a later date be helpful? What would be helpful for you right now?'*

Listening includes asking more questions

As they share their experiences, listening involves asking more questions. Clarifying questions show interest and also provide us with more information around what they may need right now.

If they share that they are tired or exhausted, ask questions about that:

'What is contributing to your exhaustion?'

'How are you sleeping?'

'Do you have strategies for rest?'

'Do you have support?'

If they share that they are feeling overwhelmed, ask questions around what is contributing to that:

'What is on your plate at the moment?'

'Is there anything that can be reprioritised?'

'How can we support you at work during this time?'

DON'T JUMP IN WITH SUGGESTIONS AND SOLUTIONS

Our role is not to fix, solve, strategise, take action, project-manage, take over or assume responsibility for a person's mental health and wellbeing care or plan. This undermines their agency and autonomy.

It can be frustrating, uncomfortable, disappointing or upsetting to see someone struggling. We need to resist the urge to tell them what to do or try to accelerate action. It is not appropriate.

Our role is to provide a safe space for a person to share when they are struggling, check that they have a work environment of psychological safety and provide them with support in line with their needs.

LISTENING TOP TIPS

Regardless of what someone shares with you, you will be okay and be able to hold the space for them appropriately.

1. Listen to understand, not to solve.
2. Ask open-ended, neutral questions.
3. Empathise – 'I can see this is tough for you...'
4. Validate their feelings – 'I can appreciate this is a difficult time for you...'
5. Avoid judgement – no two experiences are the same.
6. Ask clarification questions.
7. Be present with their experience; don't take over with yours.
8. Don't interrupt.
9. Normalise and provide hope.
10. Don't jump in with suggestions and solutions.

CHAPTER 8

EMPOWER

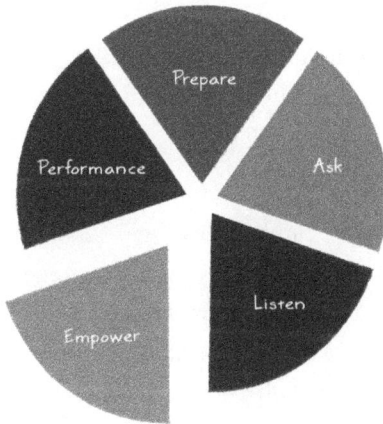

Audrey noticed that Max was struggling with workload and was often absent from work. He had previously shared with Audrey in confidence that he had been struggling with mental health issues for some time.

In their weekly one-on-one meeting Audrey shared what she had observed and asked Max how he was doing. Max opened up more about his struggles with depression and how it was affecting both his work and his personal life. Audrey thanked him for sharing his difficulties, acknowledged that things were tough for him and reassured him that mental health issues were common.

Audrey said that supporting his mental health was the priority and asked Max what kind of support he had. Max shared that he had seen a therapist in the past and found it helpful but was unsure if he wanted to go back to the therapist. Audrey asked if Max would like the help of a list of mental health resources that included therapists but also hotlines, chat forums and support groups. Max said that he would prefer to start by speaking with his doctor and seeing what he suggested.

Audrey supported Max's choice and suggested that they catch up again after his doctor's appointment so that they could incorporate any professional recommendations of how to support him at work. Audrey checked in with Max weekly to see how he was doing. Over the next two months, Max was able to find the right treatment and support system to help him manage his mental health. Eventually, Max's performance at work improved, and he was able to take on more responsibilities.

Empowering action is all about either encouraging a person to take an action that they feel comfortable with or supporting them in taking actions that they believe will assist them in their healing journey.

Key to us staying out of solving mode is to continue to ask questions and resist making suggestions.

There are four parts to empowering action and none of them involve problem-solving, fixing, project-managing or assuming responsibility for the actions that the person we are concerned for may take.

We will cover each in turn:

1. Give hope.

2. Connect to supports.

3. Encourage action.

4. Check back in.

GIVE HOPE

As a leader, normalising a person's mental health problems helps to reduce concerns they may have about stigma or job security and shows it is okay and appropriate to share their experiences with you:

> 'I am so pleased you shared with me what is going on for you. It is completely natural to experience mental health challenges.'

> 'Every year, 20% of us experience mental health issues. I am pleased you are sharing your experience with me.'

When a person is struggling with their mental health, they may feel overwhelmed or isolated and find it difficult to be proactive in taking steps towards recovery. As leaders, we can give hope and provide encouragement:

> 'Thank you for sharing what is going on for you. So many people have had a tough time these last few years; there are more support options available than ever before.'

'It's totally natural coming out of the pandemic to be feeling mental health pressure, and there are so many different options and services that are now available to you.'

CONNECT TO SUPPORTS

Just because this is the first conversation we are having with someone about their mental health doesn't mean that they aren't speaking with others and aren't already accessing support:

'I'm sorry to hear that you're not travelling so well at the moment. Do you have any support?'

There are two important sources of support to check in with – professional support for their mental health, and social support for their mental wellbeing and healing journey:

'Have you spoken to anyone about how you are feeling, such as family, a close friend or your GP?'

If they do have support outside work, it is also helpful to offer support at work:

'How can we support you at work?'

'Does your health professional have any suggestions for how we can support you at work?'

If they don't have support or haven't accessed support, we want them to know that we are willing to help but also want to ensure that our help is welcome:

'You are dealing with a lot on your own. How can I help?'

'Have you spoken to anyone? Do you have a family member or close friend who you trust that you can speak to?'

'Do you have a GP that you could speak to about how you are feeling?'

ENCOURAGE ACTION

If they don't want to speak to us about support, it is important that we respect their autonomy and agency:

'I appreciate that you may not want to speak to me about how you are feeling, but I want you to know that if you do want to talk at any time, I am here to support you.'

If they are open to talking to us about what to do, our starting place is to encourage them to tap into strategies and steps that they are already familiar with:

'What have you tried?'

'What strategies have worked for you in the past when you have been feeling wobbly? What would be helpful for you?'

'When you have felt like this in the past, what strategies have you found helpful? Are you participating in those activities now?'

'Is there anything we can do to enable you to fully engage in those activities?'

'How can we support you?'

If they haven't felt like this before and are open to talking to us about what to do, our starting place is to ask them if they would like help with ideas for sources of support:

'I appreciate that it can be tough figuring out what to do on your own. I can help with ideas and information on support options if that would be helpful?'

'Either now or at a later time?'

We take direction for the pace of the conversation and the questions to ask based on where the person we are supporting is at, what level of support is welcome and what they find useful. We need to resist any need to rush, solve or get a commitment to take action.

Educate yourself on a range of options for help

People have different preferences for accessing help and communication. Some people will find it helpful to talk to someone they know. Other people will prefer not to share what is going on with the people that are close to them and will prefer to speak to a stranger. Some people won't want to talk at all.

So, we need to have a range of support options that we can respond with, based on the person's preference:

'Do you have a trusted family doctor that you can speak to?'

'Do you have an EAP that you can access for guidance?'

We also need to be mindful of cost and access to services. Some professional services will be prohibitively expensive for people. Access to services can also be influenced by a person's geographic location. People in regional and remote areas will have fewer options and lower confidentiality than those located in well-resourced capital cities and urban areas. Some places have supported or subsidised telehealth services, while others don't offer telehealth at all.

'Did you know that Beyond Blue has a free 24/7 helpline that you can call for guidance?'

When we are researching professional help options, we want to check there is an evidence base that supports each option's helpfulness in the treatment of mental health and that the practitioners are appropriately qualified. In Australia, a psychologist goes through a rigorous training and registration process to ensure minimum standards are met, but a counsellor does not require any qualifications. That is not to say that there aren't well-qualified, well-regarded counsellors – there are, but there are also plenty of counsellors that aren't.

> *'Did you know that the Black Dog Institute website has evidence-based fact sheets and a range of free mental health support options? That might be a good starting point for information.'*

Encourage professional support

As leaders, we are not qualified to hypothesise about or diagnose mental health problems, or prescribe solutions or treatment, so we want to encourage the person we are concerned about to speak to a professional who can.

Most people's most familiar, low-cost and accessible medical professional will be their family doctor:

> *'Do you have a family doctor? When was the last time you saw your GP? Did you know that you can talk to your doctor about your feelings, not just about how you are physically feeling?'*

> *'Did you know that your doctor can do a mental health evaluation for you?'*

If your organisation has an EAP, this is a good starting suggestion. It gives people confidential access to a trained professional, at no personal cost, who can connect them to the relevant health professional:

> *'Did you know that we have an EAP that everyone at work can access, which is a totally confidential and free option for professional help?'*

'The EAP may be a good place to start in getting professional ideas and suggestions for help that are relevant to what you are experiencing.'

I also encourage you as a leader to use the EAP as a confidential source of guidance and support that you can access when you want help with strategies for supporting someone you are concerned about.

There are professional not-for-profit organisations such as Beyond Blue and the Black Dog Institute that also provide free helplines and crisis lines for people who want anonymity or to ensure confidentiality from work or family. They also have free online diagnostics, resources for self-help, text-based services, AI chat and community chat forums for people who would like more information but don't want to speak to someone.

Encourage social support

Our social support network is an important protective factor for mental health and an important promoting influence for our wellbeing. Even having just one support person outside of work, alongside their health professional, can have a positive impact on someone's healing journey:

'Have you spoken to your partner about this?'

'Do you have someone in your family who you can speak to?'

'Do you have a close friend who you can share how you are feeling with?'

What community groups are they in, or could they join some? Are they part of a sporting team, or is there a special-interest group they could join, such as a book club? Is there someone who they could speak with there?

CHECK BACK IN

Regardless of whether someone wants your help or not, it is important that you check back in with them to see how they are going. This demonstrates that you really want to know how they are and that your offer of support is genuine.

For people who are reluctant to talk, it may take asking how they are three, five or ten times before they realise that you really want to know how they are, are ready to make the time and are willing to listen.

For those who have shown trust and vulnerability, checking back in with them shows that you are interested in their care and are genuine about your offer of support.

For people who are struggling to take action, knowing that they have encouragement and a supporter can make the difference between them finding the courage and energy to get to a professional appointment and not.

So, let them know that you would like to check back in with them:

'Is it okay if I check back in with you? I would like to see how you are going at the end of the week.'

'Can I check back in with you in a couple of days to see how you went at your doctor's appointment?'

'Can I check back in with you after your EAP call to see if there is anything they recommend that we can support you with at work?'

And when you check back in again, utilise neutral, open-ended questions:

'How have you been feeling since we last spoke?' (not *'Have you been feeling better?'*)

'How did you find the Beyond Blue information?'

'Have you had a chance to speak to your doctor? How are you feeling after speaking to your doctor?'

'Did your doctor suggest anything that we can help you with?

Did the doctor suggest how we can support you at work?'

'Are there any other supports we can help with?'

EMPOWER ACTION TOP TIPS

Empowering action is about encouraging the person you are concerned about to connect with professional and social sources of support.

1. Normalise that what they are feeling is natural.
2. Give hope that there is a range of options for support.
3. Check to see what strategies and supports they may already be accessing.
4. Be literate in a range of support options.
5. Encourage and support them to connect to professional help: doctors and therapists, helplines and online self-care tools such as websites and chat forums.
6. Encourage them to access social supports such as family, friends, and community and support groups.
7. Check back in and demonstrate your support is genuine.

CHAPTER 9

PERFORMANCE

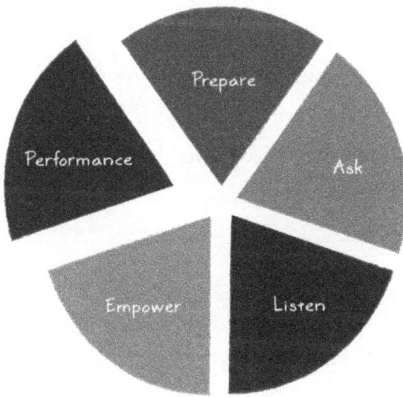

Jane was a new leader for a health care centre and had been promoted to a different location with responsibility for a larger team. The team had three vacancies that it was recruiting for, with most staff taking on additional responsibility and hours to cover the workload.

Jane observed over a period of two months that one of her team members, James, had a pattern of calling in at least one morning each week with unplanned sick leave.

Then, on the days that James attended work, he was late, left his shift early and took extensive cigarette breaks. The frustration and resentment was boiling over with the rest of the team and poisoning morale.

Jane organised a meeting with James to discuss her concerns with his performance. James was shocked and surprised to hear there were problems. He told Jane that his previous manager hadn't raised any problems with either his performance or work hours, which had been flexible for two years in support of his mental health issues.

There was no documentation of a recent performance review or support plan for James in the previous manager's notes. Jane came to one of my leadership workshops wanting to know what she could do.

Jane's situation is all too familiar. Many leaders wanting to do the right thing by a struggling team member prioritise mental health support at the expense of performance. They then find that the drop in productivity has gone on for so long that they don't know how to address the need for performance to improve.

Other leaders avoid the mental health check-in conversation but also avoid discussing performance. They don't know what to say and hope that the issue will naturally be resolved over time, and then they find that performance does not improve fast enough or at all.

Then there are leaders who focus on performance management and ignore potential mental health problems. Putting additional pressure on a person who is already struggling may contribute to a deterioration in their mental health and productivity, and may result in a long leave of absence and expensive workers compensation claims.

BALANCING CARE WITH PERFORMANCE

The most common question I get from leaders is how to appropriately manage a team member who is struggling with mental health problems and deteriorating performance.

By initiating a conversation when we first notice the signs of struggle, showing the person empathy and respect and offering support, we are creating the foundations for a positive rather than negative performance discussion.

There are four helpful principles to consider, and we will cover each in turn:

1. Make wellbeing part of your everyday conversations and meetings.
2. Separate the care conversation from the performance conversation.
3. Ensure clarity around confidentiality and team communication.
4. Create a positive performance discussion.

MAKE WELLBEING PART OF YOUR EVERYDAY CONVERSATIONS AND MEETINGS

The best way to break down any awkwardness we may feel as leaders checking in with a team member we are concerned about is to normalise checking in on wellbeing as part of our everyday conversations. It doesn't require extra effort, just better utilising of the meetings we already hold each week.

Here are some ideas for how to do this:

- Try starting your weekly one-on-one meetings by asking the person how they are, not just what they are doing. Ask them what is working well for them and also what they are feeling challenged by. Make it a routine part of your agenda to ask them what help they need.

- With team meetings at the beginning of the week, ask each team member to share a highlight from their weekend, what their top priority for the week is and what support they need from the team.

- With team meetings at the end of the week, invite each team member to share something they feel grateful for and something they have learned, and to thank another team member for something they helped with during the week.

When wellbeing is part of the everyday team culture, it will be easier for you to share what you have noticed and bring up your concerns with someone who isn't travelling so well.

SEPARATE THE CARE CONVERSATION FROM THE PERFORMANCE CONVERSATION

When we have action-oriented, solution-focused work and project meetings in which efficiency is important, we may also carry this mindset into our people-development conversations.

Alex organised a one-on-one meeting with Jasmine for the end of the week.

Over the past two months, Alex had noticed that Jasmine was tired and had become increasingly withdrawn. She had stopped joining the team for social lunches and snapped at people when they followed her up to participate.

Jasmine had been forgetting important team meetings, missing project deadlines and making silly errors in work that she knew how to do well. In Alex's most recent executive meeting, Jasmine had embarrassed the team by presenting their annual strategy for budget approval with contradicting recommendations.

As the scheduled meeting time got closer, it became clear that Jasmine was struggling personally, but the list of performance issues was also growing. Alex was dreading the meeting and feeling conflicted about how to show personal care while also addressing the need for performance improvement.

To set you and the person you are concerned about up for a successful connecting conversation, it will help you to focus on just one core issue at a time. Plan for a care conversation, and then, when care support is in place, talk about performance support.

This will take pressure off you and enable you to show up authentically for each conversation. It will also provide more psychological safety and show consideration for them. Mental health safety and care is the first priority.

Start with psychological safety and the care conversation.

Alex invited Jasmine to catch up for a coffee at a café rather than talk in the office's formal meeting room. As they walked to the café, Alex asked Jasmine what she had been reading with her book club over the last month, something that they knew she did to relax. Jasmine shared that she hadn't been in the head space to be able to read over the past few weeks.

When they had ordered their coffees and sat down at a table, Alex shared that they were concerned about Jasmine and provided some specific examples about her tiredness and withdrawing from social activities. Jasmine started to get defensive about her performance.

Alex established the context by assuring Jasmine that this was an informal conversation about her wellbeing and to see how the team could support her. Jasmine relaxed slightly but froze until Alex went on to reassure her by clarifying that this was not a performance discussion – this was a wellbeing chat. Alex went on to say that the priority was to support her wellbeing and that they would talk at a later date about how they could work together to support her performance.

When we start the care conversation, it is important to let the person know that we will also talk about supporting their performance at some stage.

If it is clear to you that there are performance issues, it is also likely that they will be stressing about their struggles at work. So, we need to address the elephant in the room at the outset. With our framing, we make it clear that our intent for addressing their performance issues is positive:

> *'We will work together to support your performance during this time.'*

Then, be patient. It is okay for the care conversation to be paced and held over a few conversations before you start discussing performance.

ENSURE CLARITY AROUND CONFIDENTIALITY AND TEAM COMMUNICATION

Unless you are concerned for your team member's immediate physical safety, your starting principle is to provide them with a commitment of confidentiality.

Confidentiality includes not sharing their personal information with anyone else or writing file notes for yourself about what they have shared that could be accessed by someone else without their express permission.

If your team member is comfortable sharing with you what is going on, you will be better able to support them. However, they are under no obligation to disclose what they are experiencing personally – and we know that there are a whole bunch of reasons, including the fear of stigma, as to why they may not want to disclose what is going on for them. The more psychological safety they feel with us, the more likely they are to share.

If they choose not to disclose their mental health challenges to you and you are still concerned:

- ask if there is any assistance or adjustments that could assist them in performing their job
- let them know you are there to listen at any time
- offer confidential external support from your EAP
- let them know that you would like to check back in again with them at an appropriate time.

If they disclose their mental health challenges with you, you must keep their personal details confidential unless they agree for you to disclose their information to another person.

If they share with you their mental health issues, discuss together what will and won't be shared with their team members and colleagues. The more they disclose to others, the more opportunities there will be for the team to provide support but also the greater the personal risk to them of being judged and treated differently.

If they elect for complete confidentiality, you must respect that and provide minimal communication. It might be as simple as advising the changes you have discussed:

> 'Jasmine has been asked to change her work duties for a specific period to focus on the following tasks, which she has agreed to.'

CREATE A POSITIVE PERFORMANCE CONVERSATION

Most people experiencing mental illness will be able to perform most of the requirements of their job when provided with flexibility and support at work. Rather than stressing over the errors and issues that you have identified, try approaching the conversation with a frame of compassion and collaboration.

Assume the best rather than the worst. Instead of documenting the gaps and what a person can't do, create a performance plan focusing on what they can do, with agreed timeframes, and what support you will provide them.

Alex and Jasmine created a mental health support plan that included regular check-ins, flexible work hours and access to the confidential EAP.

The following week Alex scheduled a performance discussion with Jasmine. Alex wanted to discuss her workload, how she felt about completing her core tasks and how the team could support her in achieving her goals.

Alex opened by acknowledging how much they appreciated Jasmine's contribution to the team and how important she was to the success of their projects. Then, Alex asked Jasmine how she was feeling and if there were any changes to her mental health that they needed to be aware of.

Jasmine shared that she was doing well, but she had been struggling with the pressure and anxiety of meeting the deadlines of an urgent, high-profile team project. Alex listened attentively, asked clarifying questions and asked Jasmine if there were any other aspects of her role that she was concerned about.

Jasmine felt confident and comfortable in managing the rest of her workload if she could get help with the priority project. Alex asked Jasmine what project support would be helpful for her. Jasmine asked if the timeline could be extended by a week and if it was possible to get some administrative support for the executive team presentation. She also asked that the team not be told about her mental health challenges.

The timeline wasn't negotiable, but some of her other duties could be delegated for the upcoming week. Support was allocated to her for creating the presentation, and they organised a time for Jasmine to practise delivering the presentation in advance the following week.

Alex and Jasmine documented her agreed performance plan for the upcoming month, noting the priorities, timelines, check-ins and extra support provided. They agreed to review her progress in four weeks' time.

In the next team meeting, Alex shared that Jasmine's focus for the month was the project and asked the team to help her out with her other duties.

POSITIVE PERFORMANCE CONVERSATION FRAMEWORK

1. **Focus on what they can do:** Start with their position description and agree together what the core requirements of the team member's job are that need to be completed. Discuss each requirement and assess together the team member's ability to perform that aspect of their job. Both of you provide a rating from 1 to 5 for each and talk through any differences in what you have selected.

2. **Discuss their strengths as well as their gaps:** Focus the conversation on what they can do and what support they need to successfully deliver what they feel confident with. Then look at what they are less confident in delivering and whether those tasks can be delayed, postponed or delegated for a period of time, or have their deadlines extended.

3. **Discuss reasonable adjustments:** Start with their ideas. They may not need adjustments, just more regular check-ins and feedback. Look more broadly for good ideas – what adjustments have worked well for others who have experienced similar situations? Incorporate any professional and medical recommendations they have received (if shared with you) for how they could be supported at work.

4. **Collaborate on confidentiality and team communication:** Agree on what information will and won't be shared with their colleagues. The less that is shared, the less work it is reasonable for the team to pick up; not sharing may reduce the reasonable adjustment options available.

5. **Be clear on timeframes for support:** In our case study with James from the beginning of this chapter, the biggest challenge Jane faced in requesting performance improvement was a lack of clarity, feedback and documentation of performance expectations. You might like to start with trialling the changes and supports for one month, and then organise a time to discuss what is working, what isn't and what might need to be adjusted.

6. **Agree on regular check-in and performance review dates:** Frequent check-ins and touchpoints will help you both to course-correct as required. A quick catch-up at the beginning of the week to confirm priorities helps with focus. A check-in at the end of the week gives you both the opportunity to provide feedback on what is working and whether any changes are needed.

7. **Create documentation:** As it is important to support confidentiality around their mental health issues, your documentation covers what they can do, their agreed performance plan and time period, the progress they are making and the supports you are providing.

8. **Undertake a longer-term review:** Once reasonable adjustments have been made and support provided, and a reasonable period of time has passed, objectively assess together whether your team member can meet the ongoing requirements of their job. In the event that they are unable

to perform the duties they were employed to do, and other options for redeployment aren't available, you have the appropriate documentation to take the next steps.

BALANCING CARE AND PERFORMANCE TOP TIPS

1. Make wellbeing part of your everyday conversations and meetings.
2. Separate the care conversation from the performance conversation.
3. Create a positive performance discussion.
4. Focus on what they can do.
5. Incorporate reasonable adjustments and supports.
6. Be clear with communication, confidentiality and timeframes.
7. Schedule regular check-ins and formal review dates.

MENTAL HEALTH MASTERY

**Leading wellbeing is about doing the right thing
for both your people and the organisation.**

I led a homewares business through two years of global financial crisis, during which every morning I was greeted by the stressed faces and anxious questions of the factory and warehouse people who worried about their job security.

I was given a directive to reduce headcount by 30%. I knew that this was not the right thing to do by the loyal staff, many of whom had worked for the business in excess of 20 years and didn't have the skills to find alternative employment in a country that no longer valued manufacturing. I also knew that it wasn't the right thing for the business, because the factory production lines weren't run on percentages. They were run by teams with people in dedicated positions. Reducing 30% of the workforce meant that we would only be able to operate at 50% production, not allowing us to fulfill the increase in orders when sales eventually improved.

I fundamentally believe that if you do the right thing by your people, they will do the right thing by you.

I came up with an alternative strategy, which was to ask my staff to work with me to balance the financials that we needed to provide to the board by working reduced hours. The legal advice was that I needed every individual to personally agree to the reduction in hours. If just one person said no, it would trigger a mass redundancy offer that the business couldn't afford.

I called a meeting with the factory and warehouse team and, absolutely petrified at the sea of faces staring at me, started my shaky request. Calls immediately came up from the floor saying, 'louder', 'we can't hear you' and 'we can't see you'.

So, I climbed up and stood on the top of a canteen-room table to ask people to trust me, that I had a plan for all people to have some work, and that we would figure out together how we would support each other during this tough time. When I finished my impassioned speech, the room went deathly quiet. Then, in small groups, people started translating what I had for their non-English-speaking co-workers, who were waiting expectantly.

Three of the leaders of the larger groups came together, spoke, and then stepped forward. They said:

> *'We don't really understand what you said, but we trust you. If you believe this is the right way and need each of us to work less and sign the form, we will do it. We trust that you care about us and believe this is the best way.'*

Then every single person formed a line behind my table. Every single person signed the paper and thanked me. I held back my tears and thanked each one of them for being willing to try another way.

Not only did we keep people's jobs, we also overperformed commercially in a tough market. The Group Managing Director said:

> *'In her role as CEO, Fleur impressed me with her ability to both develop the business strategically for the long term and also consistently deliver a strong operational and profit performance. She capably managed not only the normal pressures of the business but the situational emergencies as they occurred. It was with admiration that I saw her handle quickly and effectively a company restructure, renegotiate customer trading agreements, address individual people issues, increase market share and with our smallest company post the best profit of the whole group during the GFC.'*

People who are well do well.

SO, LET'S NOW BRING TOGETHER EVERYTHING WE HAVE LEARNED

Mental health conversation competence helps to strengthen your relationships with your team, leading to improved communication, collaboration and overall performance.

1. Start by providing an everyday foundation of psychological safety

Psychological safety is a shared belief held by all members of a team that interpersonal risk-taking is safe within the team. All members of our team feel welcome, included and accommodated on our bus.

We know we have a psychologically safe team when descriptors such as those in Table 10 are used.

Table 10: Descriptors when psychological safety is present

accepting	appreciative	clear
cohesive	connected	constructive
empowering	engaging	fair
flexible	friendly	inclusive
just	listened to	motivating
open	positive	respectful
rewarding	safe	straightforward
supportive	tolerant	trusting
valued	welcoming	worthwhile

We know we have work to do on psychological safety with our team if descriptors such as those in Table 11 are used.

Table 11: Descriptors when psychological safety is absent

aggressive	combative	confusing
discriminatory	disrespectful	draining
exclusionary	exhausting	ignored
inconsistent	isolating	micromanaging
negative	over-controlling	overwhelming
stigmatising	stressful	tense
tough	toxic	uncaring
unfair	unmanageable	unrealistic
unsafe	unsupportive	valueless

2. Get clear on what your role is and isn't

While there is no one-size-fits-all set of policies, guidelines and regulations, there are some guiding principles that will support leaders to appropriately check in and support, rather than assume responsibility for someone experiencing mental health challenges (see Table 12).

Table 12: Defining our leadership role

Our role is	Our role is not
To notice the signs when someone isn't travelling well and check in.	To problem-solve or fix, or to take over or assume responsibility for their recovery.
To provide psychological safety so everyone on our team feels accepted and able to bring their whole self to work and take interpersonal risks.	To ensure team members conform to group preferences and comfort norms.
To provide privacy and confidentiality to support team members who may be struggling to reach out and ask for help, and to encourage them to access appropriate professional supports.	To share someone's mental health issues with others without their permission.

Our role is	Our role is not
To provide reasonable adjustments to support their participation and performance at work to the best of their ability.	To diagnose or judge what a person does or doesn't need, or can or can't do.
To ensure people aren't discriminated against.	To make unilateral changes to a person's tasks, workload or role, or threaten their job security.

3. Check in at the early signs of stress, burnout and mental health issues, and offer support

As leaders, it is important that we support people in having good mental health at work. This means providing a healthy environment and playing an active role in managing the work causes of stress and burnout before they get out of hand.

When we see someone struggling, we need to reach out and make the effort to connect. Research shows that early support for someone exhibiting signs of stress, distress or struggling to cope improves their health outcomes.

We don't need to know what their specific reasons are for struggling or not feeling safe enough to reach out for help; we just need to know that stigma and barriers exist – and be prepared to make the first move.

The signs are obvious if we look for them (see Table 13).

Table 13: See the signs checklist

Changes	Signs
Physical differences	Appearance Energy Sleep Physical ailments Weight
Emotional intensity	Distress Erratic Excessive mood swings Withdrawal Conflict
Behavioural pattern changes	Attendance Effort Quality Quantity Timeliness
Period of time changes observed for	Day Week Weeks Month Months

4. Use the Mental Health Mastery Framework to support you to have better conversations

There are five steps to building your conversation competence and confidence (see Figure 5):

1. **Prepare:** Plan your approach and what to say.

2. **Ask:** Start the conversation.

3. **Listen:** Show empathy and understanding.

4. **Empower:** Encourage action without taking on responsibility.

5. **Performance:** Balance care with performance conversations.

Figure 5: The Mental Health Mastery Framework

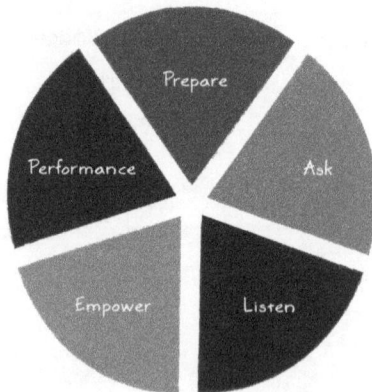

5. Positively manage both the care and the performance conversations

Most people experiencing mental illness will be able to perform most of the requirements of their job when provided with flexibility and support at work. Use the positive performance conversation framework to create a performance plan focusing on what they can do, with agreed timeframes, and what support you will provide them:

1. Focus on what they can do.

2. Discuss their strengths as well as their gaps.

3. Discuss reasonable adjustments (reasonable for them as well as for the team) and incorporate any professional and medical recommendations.

4. Collaborate on confidentiality and team communication.

5. Be clear on timeframes for support.

6. Agree on regular check-in and performance review dates.

7. Document what they can do, their agreed performance plan and time period, the progress they are making and the supports you are providing.

8. Undertake a longer-term review – once reasonable adjustments have been made and support provided, and a reasonable period of time has passed, objectively assess together whether your team member can meet the ongoing requirements of their job.

*

The Mental Health Mastery Framework provides you with the appropriate structure, strategies and suggested scripts to build your competence and confidence in having better conversations with your people. Supporting your people to be well will also help them to do well and ultimately achieve both healthy as well as high performance.

CONNECT WITH ME

Thank you for reading *Leading Wellbeing*. My hope in writing this book is to support your competence and confidence in having more quality mental health and wellbeing conversations at work. I also want to show you that applying the Mental Health Mastery Framework to improve the conversations you are already having will alleviate your worry and stress without adding to your workload.

I also acknowledge that making even small positive changes can be hard. And so, I encourage you to start with one small step at a time. Sustainable change takes inspiration, commitment, practice, feedback, support and accountability.

If you think that you could benefit from more focused support in improving the mental wellbeing, psychological safety and resilience of your team or organisation, get in touch for a complementary conversation and plan of action. Whether it be starting your organisational conversation with a conference keynote presentation, building your leadership team capability with a training program or providing foundational skills workshops for your staff, I can help.

If your own mental health, energy or wellbeing is feeling a little wobbly, you may want to check out my first book *Resilience Recipes: Making Space for Wellbeing that Works*. As leaders, it is important that we put on our own oxygen masks first. If we aren't at our best, we aren't going to be able to show up for our staff the way that they need us to. *Resilience Recipes* is an easy-to-read wellbeing guidebook that cuts through the sea of wellness information with a curated selection of evidence-based resilience and wellbeing strategies that are proven to work. Most of us know the basics for good physical health but don't know how to support our psychological wellbeing. This step-by-step guide covers where to start, what to do and what works for boosting your wellbeing with resilience.

I also invite you to head over to blueberryinstitute.com/resources, where will find loads of free templates, tips and other tools to support you.

I am super fortunate to do work I love with leaders and teams to leverage wellbeing and positive leadership as both people and performance advantages. To put it simply, the research now clearly shows that organisations that are well do well.

So, if you think you or your team could benefit from your own resilience recipe to get things moving along, get in touch – I would love to work with you!

Be well! Lead well!

Fleur

LET'S KEEP THIS CONVERSATION GOING!

Fleur Heazlewood

Fleur Heazlewood

Fleur Heazlewood - Be Well

hello@blueberryinstitute.com

blueberryinstitute.com

REFERENCES

CHAPTER 1: PEOPLE ARE NOT OKAY

Kitchener, B.A., Jorm, A.F. & Kelly, C.M., *Mental Health First Aid Manual*, 4th edn, Mental Health First Aid Australia, Melbourne, 2017.

National Alliance on Mental Illness, 'Mental health by the numbers', retrieved 8 May 2023, <nami.org/mhstats>.

Mental Health America, 'Adult data 2022', retrieved 24 May 2023, <mhanational.org/issues/2022/mental-health-america-adult-data>.

British Medical Association, 'Mental health pressures in England', retrieved 24 May 2023, <bma.org.uk/advice-and-support/nhs-delivery-and-workforce/pressures/mental-health-pressures-data-analysis>.

McManus, S., Bebbington, P., Jenkins, R. & Brugha, T. (eds), *Mental Health and Wellbeing in England: Adult Psychiatric Morbidity Survey 2014*, NHS Digital, Leeds, 2016.

Ministry of Health (New Zealand), 'Annual update of key results 2018/19: New Zealand health survey', 14 November 2019, <health.govt.nz/publication/annual-update-key-results-2018-19-new-zealand-health-survey>.

Wilson, A. & Nicolson, M., *Mental Health in Aotearoa: Results from the 2018 Mental Health Monitor and the 2018/19 New Zealand Health Survey*, Te Hiringa Hauora / Health Promotion Agency, Wellington, 2020.

Safe Work Australia, *Work-related Mental Disorders Profile 2015*, 2 December 2015, <safeworkaustralia.gov.au/resources-and-publications/statistical-reports/work-related-mental-disorders-profile-2015>.

Work Health and Safety Regulations 2011 (Cwlth)

Goffman, E., *Stigma: Notes on the Management of Spoiled Identity*, Simon and Schuster, 2009.

Australian Bureau of Statistics, 'National study of mental health and wellbeing', 22 July 2022 (reference period 2020–21), <abs.gov.au/statistics/health/mental-health/national-study-mental-health-and-wellbeing/latest-release>

World Health Organization, *Promoting Mental Health: Concepts, Emerging Evidence, Practice: summary report / a report from the World Health Organization, Department of Mental Health and Substance Abuse in collaboration with the Victorian Health Promotion Foundation and the University of Melbourne*, Geneva, 2004.

Health Direct, 'Good mental health', retrieved 24 May 2023, <healthdirect.gov.au/good-mental-health>.

World Health Organization, 'Mental disorders', 8 June 2022, <who.int/news-room/fact-sheets/detail/mental-disorders>.

World Health Organization, 'Occupational health: stress at the workplace', 19 October 2020, <who.int/news-room/questions-and-answers/item/ccupational-health-stress-at-the-workplace>.

World Health Organization, 'International Classification of
Diseases for Mortality and Morbidity Statistics: Eleventh
Revision', January 2023, <icd.who.int/browse11/l-m/en>.

CHAPTER 2: OUR ROLE

Murphy, M., 'Boost psychological safety on your teams with one
simple technique', *Forbes*, 24 February 2023, <forbes.com/sites/
markmurphy/2023/02/24/boost-psychological-safety-on-
your-teams-with-one-simple-technique/>.

Edmondson, A.C. & Mortensen, M., 'What psychological safety
looks like in a hybrid workplace', *Harvard Business Review*,
19 April 2021, <hbr.org/2021/04/what-psychological-safety-
looks-like-in-a-hybrid-workplace>.

Current Priorities of the U.S. Surgeon General, 'The Surgeon
General's framework for workplace mental health and wellbeing', U.S. Department of Health and Human Services,
retrieved 24 May 2023, <hhs.gov/surgeongeneral/priorities/
workplace-well-being/index.html>.

Safe Work Australia, *Model Code of Practice: Managing
Psychosocial Hazards at Work*, July 2022, <safeworkaustralia.gov.
au/doc/model-code-practice-managing-psychosocial-
hazards-work>.

Novotney, A., 'Why mental health needs to be a top priority in
the workplace', American Psychological Association, 21 April
2023, <apa.org/news/apa/2022/surgeon-general-workplace-
well-being>.

Martin, M., 'Fostering psychological safety in the workplace',
Forbes, 28 May 2021, <forbes.com/sites/forbescoachescouncil/
2021/05/28/fostering-psychological-safety-in-the-workplace/
?sh=52ac7b064773>.

CHAPTER 3: SEE THE SIGNS

Kitchener, B.A., Jorm, A.F. & Kelly, C.M., op. cit.

National Center for Biotechnology Information, 'Information about mental illness and the brain', National Institutes of Health (USA), 2007, <ncbi.nlm.nih.gov/books/NBK20369/ ?report=reader>.

Health Direct, 'Mental illness', retrieved 24 May 2023, <healthdirect.gov.au/mental-illness>.

Mental Health First Aid, 'The importance of early intervention for people facing mental health challenges', 21 June 2021, <mentalhealthfirstaid.org/2021/06/the-importance-of-early-intervention-for-people-facing-mental-health-challenges/>.

CHAPTER 7: LISTEN

Headlee, C., *10 ways to have a better conversation*, TEDxCreativeCoast, 16 February 2016, <ted.com/talks/ celeste_headlee_10_ways_to_have_a_better_conversation>.

Dwyer, F., 'Edgar Dale's cone of experience: a quasi-experimental analysis', *International Journal of Instructional Media*, vol. 37, no. 4, 2010.

RESOURCES

Beyond Blue (beyondblue.org.au): This website provides a mental health check-in to allow self-assessment of depression and anxiety, information on depressive and anxiety disorders, and contact phone numbers for those seeking help, as well as the Beyond Now suicide safety plan app.

Black Dog Institute (blackdoginstitute.org.au): The Black Dog Institute is 'the only medical research institute in Australia to investigate mental health across the lifespan'. It offers research, resources and support around mental health issues including anxiety, depression, bipolar disorder and post-traumatic stress disorder.

myCompass (mycompass.org.au): Provided by the Black Dog Institute, this is 'a customisable self-help tool for your mental health'.

Counselling Online (counsellingonline.org.au): Counselling Online is a service that provides 24/7 access to counsellors across Australia. It is provided by Turning Point, a substance-abuse treatment centre.

Lifeline 24-hour counselling and crisis support chat (lifeline. org.au/crisischat): Lifeline offers a confidential, 24/7 support service over phone, text and online chat.

First Nations Australians

Indigenous Mental Health and Suicide Prevention Clearinghouse (Australian Institute of Health and Welfare; indigenousmhspc.gov.au): Provides 'information about Aboriginal and Torres Strait Islander people's wellbeing, mental health and suicide prevention'.

Australian Indigenous Health*InfoNet* (healthinfonet.ecu.edu. au): The Australian Indigenous Health*InfoNet* is a web resource that is 'helping to close the gap by providing the evidence base to inform practice and policy in Aboriginal and Torres Strait Islander health'.

Healthdirect (healthdirect.gov.au/aboriginal-and-torres-strait-islander-peoples-mental-health): Healthdirect is the national health advice service in Australia.

Central and Eastern Sydney Primary Health Network (CESPHN; cesphn.org.au/general-practice/help-my-patients-with/aboriginal-health/). CESPHN provides information on 'the role of mainstream general practice in Aboriginal health'.

NEW ZEALAND

Mental Health Foundation of New Zealand (mentalhealth.org. nz): Mental Health Foundation is a charity providing suicide prevention, improving wellbeing and providing information and advice, campaigns and programs, and policy and advocacy.

Lifeline Aotearoa (lifeline.org.nz): Lifeline Aotearoa provides confidential, 24/7, first-contact support for all areas of mental health concern from highly trained staff and volunteers.

Hearts & Minds – Pasifika (heartsandminds.org.nz/directory-of-support-services/itemlist/category/74-pasifika): This Pacific mental health service provides cultural case support for consumers and their families, working alongside other mental health services.

UK

Mental Health UK (mentalhealth-uk.org/help-and-information): Whether you're living with a mental health condition or supporting somebody who is, this site provides up-to-date information so you can learn more about different mental health conditions or find where to get help.

Wheel of Well-being (wheelofwellbeing.org): This website provides practical information, tips and suggestions on what you can do to improve your wellbeing.

NHS Mental Health Services (nhs.uk/nhs-services/mental-health-services/where-to-get-urgent-help-for-mental-health/): This website provides a directory of where to get urgent help for mental health crises.

Mind (mind.org.uk): Mind provides information, fact sheets and links to services.

USA

Mental Health America (mhanational.org): Mental Health America is 'the nation's leading community-based nonprofit dedicated to addressing the needs of those living with mental illness and promoting the overall mental health of all … MHA's national office and its 200+ affiliates and associates around the country work every day to protect the rights and dignity of individuals with lived experience and ensure that peers and their voices are integrated into all areas of the organization'.

National Institute of Mental Health (U.S. Department of Health and Human Services; nimh.nih.gov): This US government site provides a wealth of excellent, up-to-date information on depression and suicide.

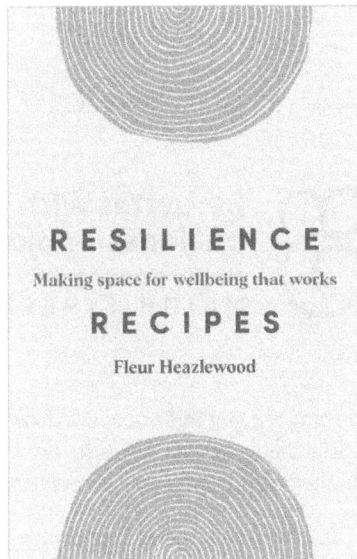

RESILIENCE
Making space for wellbeing that works
RECIPES
Fleur Heazlewood

Also by Fleur Heazlewood

Continue your wellbeing journey with the award-winning *Resilience Recipes*

To function as your best self, you need to make space for your own wellbeing. You can't help others if you don't help yourself first.

Resilience Recipes is a simple, quick-start, evidence-based guide for finding wellbeing that will work for you. It's for real people facing real-time challenges every day.

If you are feeling overworked and overwhelmed, this book will teach you the strategies to better manage stress, find more balance in your life and bounce back.

Available from all good bookstores and at majorstreet.com.au

For more information, visit resiliencerecipes.com